Quakerism
A Theology for Our Time

by
Patricia A. Williams

Copyright © 2008 by Patricia A Williams

ISBN 0-7414-4935-8

Published by:

PUBLISHING.COM

1094 New DeHaven Street, Suite 100
West Conshohocken, PA 19428-2713
Info@buybooksontheweb.com
www.buybooksontheweb.com
Toll-free (877) BUY BOOK
Local Phone (610) 941-9999
Fax (610) 941-9959

Printed in the United States of America

Printed on Recycled Paper

Published August 2008

QUAKERISM
A THEOLOGY FOR OUR TIME

TABLE OF CONTENTS

This book is dedicated to

JAY WORRALL, JR.

Quaker, author, friend

1. BACKGROUND

BIBLICAL SCHOLARS are crying out for a new paradigm for Christianity.[1] Why? Scholarship on the book of Genesis shows the doctrine of the Fall (that human nature changes for the worse) is not in the text, and this alters the atonement. Scholarship on the Gospels distinguishes sayings and deeds of the historical Jesus from those the later church created. This influences Jesus' meaning for today. Scholarship shows St. Paul thought the law superseded and, so, undermines Christian embrace of the laws in the Hebrew Scriptures, including the Ten Commandments. And, finally, documentary discoveries are altering scholarly understanding of late Judaism and early Christianity. The early church was not orthodox, but replete with a concatenation of beliefs.

Clearly, the scholarship demands that Christianity change. Blessedly, the altered paradigm scholars seek has existed since the seventeenth century. Quakers created it. Quakers based their defining belief, that all people have a measure of the divine Light within them, on experience, and their other beliefs follow logically from it.

Although this book concentrates on the Quakerism of the seventeenth century, the Quakerism I describe is alive and well in the twenty-first. I have emphasized early Quakerism to avoid confusion about whether I am referring to early or contemporary Quaker beliefs and practices. Those Quakers today known as *unprogrammed Quakers* carry on the traditions of the seventeenth century, and therefore their theology merges here with that of early Quakerism. Most of today's Quakers are orthodox Christians and thus fall under my coverage of Christian orthodoxy. Information about today's Quakers appears in appendix 1.

When referring to orthodox Christians, I mean traditions of the Catholic and Protestant West. Protestantism and Catholicism share many beliefs, for example, the Trinity, the virgin birth, the

1

divinity and two natures of Jesus (divine and human), the blood atonement, the resurrection, and salvation exclusively through Christianity. Conservatives among the orthodox also believe the Bible inerrant or read it literally and believe in Jesus' bodily resurrection and ascension. Liberals among the orthodox in the West think the early chapters of the Bible metaphorical or mythological, but read much of the remainder uncritically. They believe in Jesus' spiritual resurrection and ascension. The early Quakers emphasize spirituality – direct experience of the divine – rather than intellectual speculation. They freely criticize the Bible and find salvation through transformation of life rather than through intellectual beliefs. Therefore, they are not orthodox in either sense. They considered their movement a third way, neither Protestant nor Catholic. Quaker theologian Robert Barclay wrote their definitive work.

Robert Barclay

Robert Barclay (1648-1690) is the finest spokesperson for Quakerism's third way, even today. He was a contemporary of George Fox (1624-1691), the founder of Quakerism. Except in minor details, his theology is Fox's theology. Fox, however, although a prolific author, was largely self-educated and unsystematic in his thinking. In contrast, Barclay descended from Scottish aristocracy. He was educated in Scotland and France, in both Calvinism and Roman Catholicism. He read Greek, Latin, and Hebrew. Thus, he shocked society when he joined the Quakers in 1667 and married after the Quaker manner in the first Quaker wedding celebrated in Aberdeen, Scotland. He wrote three books. His main work, *An Apology for the True Christian Divinity,* published in Latin in 1676 and in English two years later, is so outstanding theologically and literarily that no one until now has felt the need to write another comprehensive Quaker theology, or even to update the *Apology,* except to render it in modern English.[2] In it, Barclay defends Quaker theology intellectually against the orthodoxies of his day, especially Calvinism. In an earlier work, *A Catechism and Confession of Faith* (1673),[3] he supports Quaker theology by scriptural quotation, and in *Anarchy of the Ranters and Other Libertines* (1676),[4] he defends Quaker organization against anarchy and hierarchy. For reasons that become clear in this book, Barclay's theology can thrive in the intellectual climate of the twenty-first century.

Yet, Barclay knew neither modern biblical scholarship nor contemporary science. He wrote the *Apology* a quarter century after Bishop James Ussher, through biblical scholarship, concluded that God created the world in 4004 B.C.E. and a decade before Isaac Newton's *Principia* (1687) appeared. Barclay's was a different intellectual world from our own. Barclay's original interest was to defend Quakerism as Christianity's third way against both Roman Catholicism and Protestantism. My interest is to demonstrate how well original Quaker theology fits into our contemporary intellectual climate and to contrast it, as Barclay did, with Christian orthodoxy, which Barclay deemed untenable then and certainly is unsustainable today.

Thus, the first part of this book describes Barclay's theology, the theology of early Quakerism. In doing so, it also depicts the theology underlying contemporary unprogrammed Quaker worship. Part two demonstrates that modern biblical criticism supports and even enhances early Quaker theology while undermining Christian orthodoxy. The third part shows that contemporary science also upholds and enhances early Quaker theology while early Quaker theology complements science, especially evolutionary psychology. Meanwhile, contemporary science further diminishes Christian orthodoxy. Thus, in the contemporary intellectual milieu, early Quaker theology can flourish while orthodoxy must wither.

Because the world of the early Quakers is so different from our own, it may help to situate their ideas in their own milieu, which is seventeenth century Britain.

The early Quaker milieu

When Barclay was born and Fox began to preach, Britain was embroiled in a civil war that raged from 1642-1648. It was a religious war between the monarchy in support of the established Anglican Church and the Calvinists in support of a commonwealth. For a time, the Calvinists won. They beheaded King Charles I in 1649 and established a commonwealth run by Parliament under Oliver Cromwell. It failed, and in 1660 the monarchy resumed under King Charles II. All was not well, however. Plots of various sorts fermented, persecution against dissenters (Quakers among them) became systematic, and plague and fire wracked London.

The monarchy was not secure until 1689 when William and Mary assumed the throne. Monarchy remains to this day in Britain, but between 1642 and 1689 the country transformed itself forever. Authority altered. The civil war was not the only cause. Luther posted his ninety-five theses on the door of Wittenberg Church in 1517, fomenting the Reformation.

Concurrently with the Reformation, science revolutionized the intellectual climate. Prior to Copernicus's work on the motions of heavenly bodies (1543) and Galileo's support of it (1632), authority had rested with rulers, both royal and ecclesiastical. Science questioned all authority by insisting that observation and experiment lead to truth. One of the most important voices supporting science was an Englishman, Frances Bacon, a philosopher whose *Novum Organum* (1620) praised the inductive method of arriving at truth, a method founded on observation and experiment. He also claimed, against mainstream seventeenth century thought, that knowledge accumulates. It is not merely the preservation of past wisdom. Moreover, he sought to bridge the centuries-old gap between science and technology, insisting that science is practical, not mere theory, and that technology can build upon it.

Britain began to produce great scientists. Robert Boyle (1627-1691) founded chemistry; William Harvey (1578-1657) mapped the circulation of the blood; William Gilbert (1544-1603) explored magnetism; Isaac Newton (1642-1727) bound motion on Earth and in the heavens by the same laws. Two years after the restoration of the monarchy, in 1662, the Royal Society was founded.

Yet, this was also the age of Bishop Ussher's widely accepted biblical claim that God created the world in 4004 B.C.E. More than a century passed after Ussher's proclamation before anyone speculated that Earth was older than the biblical evidence allowed. Not until the discovery of radioactivity at the end of the nineteenth century could scientists date rocks. We now know the Earth is some 4.6 billion years old, a long way from 4004 B.C.E.

The tension in the seventeenth century between science and religion appears in its poetry. John Donne's Holy Sonnet #7 (~1615) begins, "At round earth's imagined corners, blow / Your trumpets, angels." Science's Earth was round; biblical Earth had corners.

The tension is especially evident in John Milton's *Paradise Lost* (1667). This is an epic poem, patterned after the classical epics, yet totally unlike them, for the important action occurs within people rather than externally (a prominent Quaker theme!). Milton depicts Earth as unchanging after the creation and insists at some length that "whether heav'n move or earth, / Imports not" (VIII, 70-1). Yet, he describes a round Earth, linked to heaven by a golden chain (II, 1034-1053), so his Earth is partly from science, but his heaven remains a place in space. Milton conflates scientific with biblical cosmology and fears the impact of science on the trust-worthiness of the Bible.

The emerging intellectual revolution moves away from author-ity, uniformity, hierarchy, and a chain of being stretching from God to rocks, toward a world of multiplicity, disparity, and toleration. The chain of being that supported hierarchy broke, link by link, to be replaced in the middle of the nineteenth century by the image of a bush to represent organic life where species evolve from other species and none is better or worse, higher or lower, except tem-porally, some having evolved before others.

Thus, ancient authorities came under increasing attack. Fox, Barclay, and the early Quakers joined the battle. Barclay's *Apology* confronts two sources of authority. Catholics found authority in ecclesiastical hierarchy, Protestants in the Bible. Although Barclay writes his *Catechism* to demonstrate that Quakerism is more scrip-tural than Calvinism is, he rejects Protestantism's claim that the Bible is the primary authority. Barclay, following Fox, argues that the primary authority is the Holy Spirit rather than scripture. Like all those around them, Barclay and Fox believe the Bible literally: creation occurs fewer than 6,000 years ago, Adam and Eve consti-tute the first couple, Noah and his family survive a world-wide flood, the Exodus and conquest occur as the Bible describes, and Jesus is born of a virgin. Nonetheless, they treat the narratives as metaphors. Eve and Adam may comprise the first couple, but their principal importance is to provide a metaphor of human life that shows us how to live obedient to God. Like them, we are born inno-cent, but fall into sin. We need to repent and return to God. As Moses literally liberated the Jews from Egypt, so God liberates us spiritually. The original Quakers' metaphoric treatment of scrip-ture means that, when science and biblical criticism declare so much in scripture false if read literally, the Quaker theology of the seventeenth century stands firm. What mattered then, and matters now, is the Bible's inner meaning, what we now might call its spiritual import. Appendix 2 offers an updated view of metaphor and its application to seventeenth century Quaker theology.

Fox and Barclay view everything through a spiritualized, metaphoric lens. They argue against Catholicism that rituals and sacraments are useless. If they only provide outward forms, they do nothing. The Holy Spirit, not rituals or sacraments, prods the human spirit, and the Holy Spirit does not need outward rituals and sacraments to act effectively. If people do not require sacraments and rituals, they do not need clergy to perform them. Fox treats clergy unfavorably (he calls all clergy, Protestant and Catholic, priests): "But the black earthly spirit of the priests wounded my life; and when I heard the bell toll to call people together to the steeplehouse, it struck at my life, for it was just like a market-bell to gather people together that the priest might set forth his ware to sale."[5]

Authority, Barclay argues, lies not in Popes or offices or apostolic succession, but in the Holy Spirit. And he, like Fox and other early Quakers, employs many metaphors for the Spirit, the most popular being the Inward Light. In their claim for the authority of the Spirit, the early Quakers successfully accomplish what they intend, a reconstitution of the early church.[6]

The early Quakers thought the Protestant reformation accomplished much. It unseated the Pope and, among Calvinists, the bishops. It eliminated five of the seven sacraments. Yet, it made many mistakes, so many that the early Quakers did not consider themselves Protestant. Many Protestants did not judge them Protestant, either, and some accused them of not being exclusively Christian. The accusers were correct, an advantage in today's ecumenical world.

Quakers considered the central Protestant error to be failure to acknowledge the Inward Light, the Holy Spirit within everyone, and believed this failure led to the other errors. For example, the early Quakers think the Light is the primary authority, not scripture. The Light is a power acting now to show us the way to righteousness, and its revelations continue today. Calvinists believed people could not attain righteousness on Earth but were perpetually sinful in thought, word, and deed and God imputed Jesus' righteousness only to the elect, who were few indeed. They also believed revelation had ceased sometime in the second century. Quakers thought Jesus died for all people, not merely for the elect few, and they repeatedly quoted scripture to support their position, pointing out that the New Testament's good news converted to bad news for most people if the elitism of Calvinism were correct. Finally, because the Light could enlighten any and all, the Quakers allowed women to preach, whereas mainstream Christian groups limited preaching to men. Thus, the Light creates a lifestyle of equality for all people and, with it, respect for all, entailing honesty and fairness to everyone.[7]

What stands out about early Quakers is their sense – their experience – that the Holy Spirit (the inner Light) is active, here and now, and will lead all people to salvation, here and now, if they do not resist it. Quaker belief follows the New Testament. 1 Thessalonians and Acts assume the Holy Spirit is present and acts in people's lives, and prophesying was a normal activity in the early church,[8] as it was in early Quakerism. As contemporary Quaker, Lewis Benson, argues, Quakerism really does constitute a third way, rejecting institutions for unity under Christ the Light for all who obey him.[9] The question this book addresses is whether such beliefs, drawn from the New Testament as read by a small, persecuted sect in the seventeenth century, can fit into a modern intellectual framework. Can early Quaker theology remain vital now?

The current vitality of Quakerism

The West has already adopted a plethora of Quaker practices. Quakers denounced legalized slavery and freed their slaves; later, the West declared slavery illegal. Quakers preached the equality of all people; a century later, the Americans put equality into their Declaration of Independence, and the West slowly, and not yet fully, enacted it. Quakers established practical and scientific education for all men and women to replace classical education for male aristocrats; two centuries later, the West followed them. Compared with seventeenth century attire, it even adopted the plain dress of Quakers. Yet, the West failed to adopt Quaker method and theology. It turned outward to science, technology, materialism, and doctrinarism rather than inward to the spiritual life.

The authority of scripture has been under attack now for more than two centuries, both by biblical scholarship and science. We now know from cosmology and geology the Bible portrays the universe incorrectly in the creation and flood narratives and elsewhere. Archaeology tells us the Exodus and conquest, if they occurred at all, did not happen as the biblical narratives depict them. We now think the Bible is not about science and history, but about God's relationship to us, and even God changes in the text so that Jesus' God is hardly the God depicted in the flood narrative. So, why not just throw the Bible out?

Early Quakerism saves the Bible by treating its narratives as metaphors for the spiritual life, so it can teach us much – not science and history, but spirituality.

As I will argue, orthodox Christian theology is no longer tenable. Quakerism simplifies it, emphasizing spiritual experience rather than belief. Surely, as the contemporary Quaker author, John Punshon, argues, spirituality is true Christianity,[10] for without the Spirit, only dead and empty beliefs remain. A controversial nineteenth century Quaker reduced the requirements for being a Christian to three: (1) inner belief in God and Christ; (2) inner obedience to the divine will, known inwardly (rather than intellectually attained through the study of scripture); and (3) assemblies of people who love one another and produce good works.[11] Personally, I am attracted to a richer theology than this, and early Quakerism offers one that is richer while at the same time being both more experiential and more logical than Christian orthodoxy is.

In early Quakerism, biblical history frames theology. The history is peripheral while conversion is central, conversion not to belief in a particular narrative about Jesus, but to guidance by the Spirit and the transformation of one's life. Therefore, theology today can retain early Quakerism's core and place it in the new framework science offers, from the big bang, to the evolution of our species, to evolutionary psychology. Evolutionary psychology derives from the fact that we evolved and inherited dispositions from ancestors going back millions and even billions of years, rather than possessing a fallen nature inherited from Adam and Eve. Fox often writes of "people of the world" or worldliness, rather than sin. For Fox, conversion through the power of the Light is from worldliness and egocentricity to love of God and others guided by the Spirit. As I will argue, evolution made us worldly. Fox's idea of conversion from worldliness to spirituality, the transformation of our personal frame of reference, fits nicely with the central tenets of evolutionary psychology. Original Quakerism flourishes within today's scientific frame.

Finally, Quakerism emphasizes values we deeply desire: peace, cooperation, and spirituality. However, it goes further. It describes a method for achieving them, as individuals and in community. It offers both message and method. It also slips extraordinarily well into biblical scholar Marcus Borg's outline for a new paradigm in Christianity that retains God, Jesus, and the Bible, but emphasizes metaphor and experience. As Borg comments, "The notion that God is a reality who can be known (and not simply believed in) has become quite foreign in the modern world and in much of modern theology."[12] Knowing God is not foreign to Quakerism. Christianity must change to treat religion not as an addition to our lives, but as a reordering of them.[13] The original Quakerism of Fox and Barclay can help us. It is centered in experience of the divine Light within.

PART I

THE STABLE CORE: THE LIGHT WITHIN

PART I presents the central core of Quaker theology in four chapters. Respectively, the chapters discuss Quakerism from the standpoint of intellect, experience, collective action, and daily living. This stable core has not changed for more than three hundred years and requires no alteration now. It is fresh, practicable, and currently practiced in unprogrammed Quaker meetings.

2. THEOLOGY: CONSIDERING THE LIGHT

"NOW WAS I come up in spirit through the flaming sword into the paradise of God," Fox records in his Journal. "All things were new, and all the creation gave another smell unto me than before, beyond what words can utter."[14] Fox is recounting a profound religious experience. As he famously comments, "And this I knew experimentally."[15] By experimentally he meant what we today mean by experientially or existentially. Fox felt his religion. He experienced it. He did not get it second hand.

Typically, studies of the history and theology of religion in the West ignore religious experience.[16] Yet to ignore religious experience is to disregard the center of the spiritual life, not only among Quakers, but in the early church as well. In three studies,[17] James Dunn and Luke Johnson separately demonstrate that spiritual experience is fundamental for the early Christians, more fundamental than belief or dogma is. To accept baptism in the early church meant receiving the Holy Spirit as a charismatic gift, not being dipped in water. For the early Quakers, to experience the Light within was to receive the Holy Spirit, to live in Christ, to know the Father. The motive behind Quaker preaching was not to convince people of specific beliefs, but to lead them to experience the Light within for themselves.[18]

This was new. In their efforts to purify the church, the Protestant reformers subtracted rites and offices from what they perceived as the corrupt Roman Catholic system. The Anglicans eliminated the Pope, Mass, images, and five of the seven sacraments. The Presbyterians abolished bishops, the independents removed central church government, and the Quakers eradicated the liturgy and the remaining sacraments. However, the Quakers added something. They added the Light within, the experiential aspect of religion.[19] The Light they added is neither a vapid concept nor a "pale

11

intellectual illumination, but a consuming holy fire which not only revealed sin but brought you out of it."[20] This chapter concentrates on three essentials of the Light within: its divine nature, its experiential character, and its power to transform. The Light's presence within everyone is a fourth essential, but because this idea contrasts so sharply with orthodox Christianity, discussion of the universality of the Light is reserved for a separate chapter.

The Light as divine

Fox's biographer notes, and Fox insists, that the Light within is unnatural.[21] Barclay comments that the Light is not part of human nature, not a relic of goodness that remains in us as an inheritance from Adam and Eve's created state.[22] To put the unnaturalness of the Light in contemporary terms, the Light within is not a product of evolution. It did not evolve. It does not spring from our disposition to love our children and other close kin, a disposition with evolutionary roots.[23]

Opponents of the Quakers in the seventeenth century maintained that the Quaker Light was natural. Some thought it was reason. They believed that through reason we could acquire knowledge of God. Barclay denies this. He agrees that we may examine the universe and reason from our observations that it has a creator. However, study of the universe will reveal neither what righteousness is nor God's will for the individual. To understand these things, we need the Light within.[24] Moreover, Barclay continues, reason is incapable of settling controversies. Some controversies, wars, and revolts have occurred because both contending sides thought they were following proper reasoning.[25]

Reason, Barclay argues, is natural. Moreover, it can grasp some spiritual things. However, he asserts, the brain "is not the proper organ by which we know God."[26] Not that reason is useless. It has a significant role in ruling us in matters natural. Barclay offers a metaphor. God, he says, created two great lights to shine upon the Earth, the sun and the moon. Likewise, God implanted two lights in humanity, the Light within, which is divine, and reason, which is natural. As the sun illuminates the moon, the divine Light within should illuminate reason. Enlightened reason can then order human lives in matters natural and in matters spiritual, if rightly followed.[27] It is capable of making correct judgments of truth and error.[28]

Other opponents of the Quakers claimed the Quaker Light is the light of conscience. Again, Barclay disagrees. He argues that conscience is also natural. It develops in people based on the beliefs they hold, and their beliefs may be wrong. Conscience can be a false guide. As examples, Barclay cites Muslims whose consciences bother them if they drink wine, but not if they have many wives, and Catholics whose consciences suffer if they eat meat during Lent, whereas Protestants have no such qualms.[29] Barclay compares conscience to a candleholder that sheds light as long as it has a lit candle in it, but without the candle sheds no light.[30] Natural conscience is not a sound guide. It requires divine enlightenment to steer us correctly.

Interestingly, two centuries later, Charles Darwin also argues that conscience is natural. His opponents claimed natural selection could not account for it, so God must have created it. In an often-quoted passage from the *Descent of Man,* Darwin says,

> The following proposition seems to me in a high degree probable – namely, that any animal whatever, endowed with well-marked social instincts, would inevitable acquire a moral sense or conscience, as soon as its intellectual powers had become as well developed, or nearly as well developed, as in man.[31]

He then explains how conscience might have developed. The early Quakers, who knew nothing of evolution, often agree with later evolutionary thinkers. They, too, argue that conscience is natural, but add that it requires enlightenment from the divine to reveal true knowledge of good and evil.[32]

The divine nature of the Light within does not mean that it is foreign to humanity, some kind of unique insert, such as most Christian denominations believe the soul is. According to the Quakers, God permeates all that is natural and, therefore, indwells natural humanity. God's Spirit exists in natural humanity as a seed that can grow into a fully mature plant.[33] Rufus Jones, a notable Quaker author of the twentieth century, remarks that Fox carried with him an important secret: humanity is never separated from God. God is always with us.[34]

So, the Light is unnatural. It is neither reason nor conscience. What is it, then? One description is the face God turns toward humanity. We cannot know God's essence, but we can know what God reveals to us, which is all we need to know. This face God turns toward us has many names. In Christianity, it is Christ, the Holy Spirit, the Light, and the Seed. The early Quakers have many other metaphors for it: living bread, teacher, voice, peace, lamb, morning star,[35] that of God, Christ within, Word of God within the heart, witness, anointing, grace, covenant, measure, cross,[36] the life in Christ, the life in the word,[37] and, confusingly, the gospel. Quakers believe the Light dwells in everyone,[38] and because not everyone is Christian, others call it by other names: the Buddha-nature, Krishna, Atman, the Great Spirit, and the Tao, to list a few.

Barclay calls it "a spiritual, celestial, and invisible principle, a principle in which God dwells as Father, Son, and Spirit."[39] It is the source of truth, and itself infallible.[40] We, however, are fallible. Possession of the Light within does not lead to infallibility. Thus, although the Light is infallible, we may be mistaken about what we report about it or what it has told us to be or to do. The early Quakers did not claim infallibility for themselves, no matter how enlightened they felt.

Barclay makes the salient point that people, if completely natural, could never understand God. He employs another metaphor. Other animals, he says, cannot understand people because people are so much more complex or, as Barclay puts it, "higher and nobler" than other animals are. Likewise, the natural person cannot understand God because God is higher and nobler than they are, a Spirit. In order to understand God at all, people must partake in some way of the divine. The divine Light within, the Spirit of God within, alone can discern the things of God.[41]

Understandably, the concept of the Light is somewhat amorphous, but its function is unmistakable. It reproves wrongdoing, shows people how to live righteously, empowers them to live rightly, and unifies those who unite with it.[42] This Light, this principle or seed in us, directs us toward God. It is the spiritual body of Christ that feeds spiritually those who hunger for it.[43]

The Quakers' opponents pointed out, quite rightly, that many evil people exist. How, then, they asked, can all have the divine Light within them, for there is no evil in God. Barclay answers carefully that the divine dwells in people as a seed. In some, it remains undeveloped. In some, it is rejected. Like the historical Jesus, in some it is crucified. It can be, and is, resisted. However, in people who do not resist it, but receive it, it matures. And then, as it matures, "Christ is resurrected and takes shape as the new man which the scriptures so often speak of. . . . This is the Christ within of which we speak so often."[44] Here early Quakerism's Christian roots show clearly. The Light within is Christ. Yet, for the early Quakers, Christ is an eternal principle, the uncreated, eternal Logos that dwelled fully in the historical Jesus. Its presence in us does not depend on Jesus' resurrection.[45]

Barclay says the Light within is the gospel, but the gospel is neither an assertion nor an announcement. It is a power, the saving power of God, a power within people that teaches them and reveals what is good.[46] Fox knows this power. "He knew Christ, not as a theological truth, not as a comfortable emotional experience, but as a divine power able to shatter sin's dominion over man."[47] Fox and Barclay know this power from experience.

The Light as experiential

In his work on religious experience in early Christianity, Luke Johnson comments, "Religious experience is a response to that which is perceived as ultimate, involving the whole person, characterized by a peculiar intensity, and issuing in action."[48] He continues by explicating this definition. Religious experience is a response. The recipient does not initiate it. The person who has the experience feels it is ultimate rather than relative, that it is valuable in itself. The whole person responds, not only the mind, but also feeling and will. The response is one of both attraction and fear. The experience is intense, a peak experience. However, it is not necessarily dramatic, but may occur in quiet meditation. Finally, it results in action. It transforms people so they organize their other activities around it. Johnson ends by noting that specific religions are ways to organize and mediate this transforming power.[49]

Fox, however, thinks specific religions are often ways to resist this transforming power, which is why he is so critical of both Protestantism and Catholicism. He sees the Light within and the gospel as the power of God[50] and thinks this power is in the heart,[51] that is, more in the emotions than in the intellect, although he probably has in mind what Johnson means by the whole person.

Barclay agrees. He thinks true knowledge of God comes only through the "Spirit shining in upon the heart, enlightening and

opening the understanding" and not by intellect.[52] He writes that
the Spirit reveals itself in diverse ways, by "outward voices and
appearances, dreams, or inward objective manifestations in the
heart"[53] and that it speaks to the inward person rather than the
outer ear.[54] He develops a metaphor. He explains that little children who can see know the light of the sun and colors because they
experience them directly, whereas blind adults cannot know them,
even after the most trenchant explanations. So it is with the Spirit.
The most incisive explanations will not teach people to understand
the Spirit, but direct experience of it edifies them so thoroughly
that it obliterates the question of whether they have really encountered it. To people who have experienced the Spirit, the question
of how they know they experienced it becomes as foolish as asking
sighted people how they know the sun is shining at noon.[55]

The experience is of something eternal – God, the eternal
Christ, the Logos, the Holy Spirit. Fox says the Spirit was present
before Jesus was born, before scripture was written, from the beginning.[56] Barclay comments that Noah and Abraham, who lived
before the scriptures were written, acted through the Spirit.[57] He
remarks that when St. Paul says in 1 Corinthians 10:3-4 of those
traveling with Moses, "And all ate the same spiritual food, and all
drank the same spiritual drink. For they drank from the spiritual
rock that followed them, and the rock was Christ,"[58] Paul is referring to the spiritual Christ who preexists Jesus.[59] Therefore, experience of the Spirit does not depend on its incarnation in Jesus or
on his resurrection.

The New Testament emphasizes religious experience more than
other ancient religious texts do.[60] For St. Paul, grace is an experience, not a belief.[61] Barclay quotes Paul on the inwardness of the
Spirit that Paul could have known only by his own, personal experience of its power. Paul says, "But you are not in the flesh; you are
in the Spirit, since the Spirit of God dwells in you" (Rom. 8:9a)
and "Do you not know that your body is a temple of the Holy Spirit
within you, which you have from God?" (1 Cor. 6:19). Barclay finishes by quoting Romans 8:9b, "Anyone who does not have the
Spirit of Christ does not belong to him," and observes that Paul
did not think a person without the experience of the indwelling
Spirit was a Christian.[62]

Fox and Barclay do not think the Spirit ceased its activity with
the canonization of the New Testament, as many Protestants

believe. Fox considers himself and his followers ministers of Christ. He remarks, "And therefore none can be a minister of Christ Jesus but in the eternal Spirit, which was before the Scriptures were given forth."[63] Against the Protestant view that prophecy ceased with the closing of the New Testament canon, he wryly observes that prophecy has ceased only in people who are blind to the presence of the Light.[64]

Both Fox and Barclay equate the inner experience of the Light with baptism and communion, a baptism and communion without the outward vehicles of water, bread, or wine. For those who experience the Light, baptism and communion occur inwardly, in a fiery and tender relationship with the Spirit. Rex Ambler, who has studied the early Quakers extensively, notes that the experience of the Quakers is sufficiently different from normal, everyday experience that Quakers require a language of transcendence, a language of Spirit, Christ, and God, to talk about it.[65]

The early Quakers must have had many, diverse spiritual experiences in their silent (and sometimes not so silent) meetings. However, the prevailing experience seems to be a version of a life review in which people see their sins – and weep in repentance of them – but also see their salvation. The Light within, says Fox, shows us our sins, but we need to look over our sins to the Light that also brings purification, peace, and knowledge of God to us.[66] Modern Quakers say similar things. Howard Brinton comments that the Light within is a source of knowledge of good and evil and of religious truth.[67] John Punshon declares the Light searches us and heals us, and that we need to become aware of our vices.[68]

The Quakers do not have a second-hand religion. Barclay the scholar does not think religious knowledge comes from scholarship.[69] Fox the preacher does not think it comes from preaching. In fact, the goal of his ministry is to end all outward preaching.[70] Nor does spiritual knowledge come from the Bible. Famous is Margaret Fell's report of Fox's preaching, "'You will say, Christ saith this, and the apostles say this; but what canst thou say?'"[71] Here Fox is criticizing those who preach from the Bible according to their own lights rather than preaching from the Light within them. Unlike them, Fox receives his religious knowledge first-hand from the Light, not from scripture. He sees inwardly that the Light of Christ enlightens everyone, but some hate and reject it, even though they profess to be Christian. "This," he says, "I saw in the pure openings of the Light without the help of any man, neither did I then know where to find it in the Scriptures. . . . For I saw in that Light and Spirit which was before Scripture was given forth . . . which they that gave them forth were led and taught by."[72]

Barclay remarks that knowledge of the historical Jesus profits us little. We need to experience the Spirit.[73] He thinks that to say the correct words, "Jesus is Lord," without the Spirit is to be like an actor – or a parrot![74] As Barclay correctly points out, many truths are not in Scripture, especially truths that apply to particular institutions and individuals. To attain these truths, we require direct spiritual enlightenment.[75] He also notes that, ultimately, all Christian beliefs depend on the Holy Spirit. Catholics say things worthy of belief come from the church and its traditions, but when asked for the reason, they say because the Spirit leads the church infallibly. Protestants say the scriptures tell them what to believe, but when asked why, they say God revealed the scriptures inwardly by the Spirit to the people who wrote them.[76]

The Light the Quakers encounter seems to be the same Light people see who undergo near death experiences. Particularly interesting are children who have near death experiences because their cultures have not influenced them to the same extent culture shapes adults. Nearly all children and about one-fourth of the adults who have near death experiences perceive a Light. And not only a Light. They experience love, warmth, forgiveness, beauty, peace, joy, and wholeness or oneness with the universe. Some hear voices they equate with the voice of God. Their experiences transform their lives,[77] much as the experiences of the early Quakers transformed theirs.

The Light as transformative

Early Christians linked spiritual experiences with morally transformed lives,[78] as do the seventeenth century Quakers, Barclay[79] and Fox, and the twentieth century Rufus Jones[80] and Thomas Kelly.[81]

Fox, of course, thinks in biblical terms. He views all people as sharing the sinful nature of the fallen first couple, himself included. However, God/Christ raises him in a profound religious experience from that sinful state to the innocent state of Adam before the Fall.

Now was I come up in spirit through the flaming sword into the paradise of God. All things were new, and all the creation gave another smell unto me than before, beyond what words can utter. I knew nothing but pureness, and innocency, and righteousness, being renewed up into the image of God by Christ Jesus, so that I say I was come up to the state of Adam which he was in before he fell. . . . But I was immediately taken up in spirit, to see into another or more steadfast state than Adam's in innocency, even into a state in Christ Jesus, that should never fall.[82]

Fox's thought here is that Adam, although innocent, when tempted fell into sin. Jesus, also innocent, when tempted resisted sin. Fox's sense is that he is not only innocent as Adam was, but able to resist temptation as Jesus was. And, indeed, Fox seems to have resisted it or, better yet, not to have felt tempted in alluring circumstances. Other early Quakers were similar. Fox reports being invited to dine with Cromwell's aristocratic friends, but Fox refuses. When Cromwell hears of Fox's rebuff, he declares the Quakers are the only people in the land he cannot win over with honors, offices, or bribes.[83] Barclay writes of being freed from "disordered passions and lusts"[84] and saved from worldly pursuits to live thoughtfully and soberly.[85]

Their comments deserve translation into contemporary terms. It is clear now that we have evolved to have certain basic dispositions, fundamental inclinations to pursue resources, reproduction, reciprocity, and caring for relatives more than we care for those not closely related to us. Without such inclinations, our species would have gone extinct.[86] Yet, pursuit of them is worldly, and too vigorous pursuit of them leads to classical sins such as greed, lust, deception, and nepotism. Fox and Barclay are suggesting that the Light within, the power of the divine Spirit, can remove people from worldliness and wrongdoing, if they want to withdraw, and lead them to a state in which worldliness and evil no longer tempt. Instead, people lead lives with serious purposes, lives devoted to the welfare of others, lives characterized by love and compassion.

Another way to translate their perspective from the seventeenth century is to see through the eyes of modern psychology. A modern student of mysticism, Emma Shackle, says mystical experience produces changes in people that resemble Karl Jung's state of individuation, in which people become whole.[87] The Quaker Kelly writes of two levels of mental life, a superficial one concerned with external things, and a deeper one close to the divine that makes people whole, enhances creativity, and induces a state of joy and peace the superficial mind cannot grasp. Spiritual experience pulls the shallow mind down into the deeper level, where people reassess petty pursuits and reorder their lives.[88]

The New Testament tells of experiences of power – not the external powers of rank, status, wealth, or weapons – but a power that transforms people internally when it touches them. This transcendent power offers intimacy and communication with the Spirit, an active power that indwells, moves, transforms, and gives new life. It is a power that is poured upon people and into them, bringing them into a world full of Spirit.[89]

Barclay perhaps sums up the transformation most simply. He suggests the metaphor of people in love who constantly remember the beloved while they are eating, working, and playing, who avoid at all cost doing anything that might affront the beloved. All, Barclay says, should love God like this.[90]

Such love alters our perceptions. Barclay writes of people using only their natural minds who see laws as external and literal,[91] whereas spiritual people experience an internal law and view the external laws as metaphors. Fox writes of his body being changed, of becoming innocent, and of people who once condemned others suddenly seeing their own transgressions.[92]

Although no one can control the Light within or call up its conscious presence by will or when in need, says Barclay, it is resistible.[93] Moreover, it condemns those who resist it.[94]

Finally, Brinton observes that the true goal of religion is mystical union with the Light within,[95] while Shackle argues that quest of the mystical life is not primarily the pursuit of exotic experiences, but a quest for transformation.[96] Surely the mystical life is both, and each is handmaid to the other. Uniquely, Quakers pursue the experience of Light and the transformed life communally through silent group worship.

3. WORSHIP: EXPERIENCING THE LIGHT

SO, THE CORE beliefs of early Quaker theology are that the Light is divine, experiential, transformative, and within everyone. Logically, if the Light has these characteristics, we can and should attend to it. We should because it is divine and therefore important. We can because it is experiential. Moreover, to lead lives conformed to the Light, divine lives, we naturally evolved human beings require transformation. The Quaker way of worship follows logically from this core Quaker theology. In worshiping together, Quakers turn inward to the Light, maintain silence, and avoid external distractions. As Brinton notes, if the Spirit reveals itself directly to us, then logically we should wait patiently for its revelation.[97] Waiting for a revelation of the divine is what Quakers do in Meeting for Worship. Because the Light is within everyone, and may reveal itself to anyone at anytime, if anyone in Meeting feels moved to deliver a vocal message from the divine to the group, that person may (and should) do so.

As George Gorman rightly notes, Quaker worship involves the whole personality, and to understand it is to understand the Quakers.[98] Thus, this examination of the early Quaker way of worship will further illuminate early Quaker theology. Nonetheless, a caveat. Barclay warns that proof of what occurs in Quaker Meetings rests not on logical arguments, but on experiencing for oneself what occurs in the Meetings.[99] So, let us meet here experientially with the early Quakers in their Meeting for Worship, a way of worship that continues to this day.

Meeting in silent worship

The logic of turning inward to meet God, if the divine Light is within and available to experience, is clear enough, but opponents

21

of the Quakers often asked them why they met together if they were worshiping as individuals rather than as a collective. Why not just stay at home, enter your room alone as Jesus suggests (Matt. 6:6), and pray there? Fox answers that the Light is one and brings into unity all in whom it brightly shines.[100] Meeting together enhances the possibility of unity. Barclay says meeting together makes the inner life fuller, and then he offers a metaphor. One candle, he notes, sheds little light, whereas the more candles collected in one place, the brighter the light. Thus, each Quaker entering a Meeting brings more Light into it. Moreover, in meeting together, Quakers partake not only of the Light of Christ within themselves, but also of the Light in each other.[101] A contemporary of Fox and Barclay, Isaac Penington, proposes another metaphor. He comments that meeting together for worship is like a heap of coals. Separated, the individuals grow cold; united, the collective glows warmly together.[102]

The purpose of the Quaker Meeting for Worship, then, is to commune with God and one another. However, Quakers across the centuries have expressed this purpose in diverse ways. Brinton calls it communion, but also writes of meeting the inner Teacher and of exposure to the Light that reveals our vices.[103] He develops a modern metaphor. He compares Quaker Meeting to a scientific laboratory. Laboratory scientists withdraw from the world into a place shielded from it and perform experiments that depend on direct experience. Later, they reenter the world with the results of their experience and affect it. Meeting for Worship is like this. Quakers withdraw from the world to a place shielded from distractions. There, they conduct experiments based on direct experience, then transfer the results of their experience into the world and affect it. Brinton contrasts the scientific laboratory and the Quaker Meeting with a scientific lecture and a prepared sermon where listeners acquire information second-hand rather than through their own experience.[104] The former is better because direct and first-hand.

Barclay crafts two metaphors. He writes of Meeting where silence stills the worshipers so they can listen to God, just as attentive pupils sit still to listen to a teacher rather than talking themselves. He also compares people in Meeting to servants. The good servant awaits the Master's orders before acting. Good Quakers await God's leading hand rather than act on their own. Both the servants and the Quakers are foolish to run about doing good that is not the Master's will, rather than waiting to discover what the Master wants them to do.[105]

John Punshon is brief and biblical. "The purpose of worship is to conform us to the image of God."[106] Fox is more dramatic and metaphoric. The silence of Meeting, he writes, represents the silencing of our selves, the death of our own wisdom, so we may attend to God.[107] Expressing the heart of the New Testament, he comments, "All that worship in the spirit and truth, come to the spirit and truth in their own hearts, and [then come to] love one another and love enemies."[108] Barclay concurs. He, too, invokes love of God and neighbor.[109] He writes, "When we meet together, our purpose and our form of worship is to watch and wait for God to draw us inward and away from all visible things," to elevate good over evil, to enjoy mutual fellowship, and to exchange reciprocal aid with each other.[110]

Barclay thinks worshipers need to turn from their own thoughts and imaginations. Even if people in Meeting for Worship think about God, they are on the wrong path, for in attending to their own thoughts, they may fail to hear God. Instead, they must set aside their egocentricity and let God govern them.[111] Barclay also writes of opening oneself to God to draw strength and sustenance from the body and blood of Christ inwardly, even though no outward word is spoken or bread and wine present.[112] Truly, for Barclay, Meeting for Worship is communion with God.

Finally Barclay comments, I think wisely, that the Quaker form of silent worship does not come naturally. Rather, it grates against the grain of human nature. Therefore, it does not tempt us to worship worldly glory in place of God. Other forms of worship do tempt us because they require wealth and beautiful things of this world, imagination, and creativity. Quaker worship springs from the Spirit, whereas liturgical worship originates in human nature. We may become enamored of the mere form of liturgical worship, even though it lacks the Spirit, but Quaker worship is so plain and godly that either it takes place in the Spirit or it will cease.[113]

Because silent worship quiets and empties the mind, Quaker worship seems to resemble some practices of Eastern religions. Eastern religions use various techniques of meditation to still and empty what some call the monkey mind. In this context, Jim Pym raises the question of the relationship between Eastern meditation and Quaker worship. He observes that there are two types of meditation. The first consists of waiting for God, where God is the active party. The second promotes the meditator's own activity. He notes that, for Quakers, meditation techniques may help quiet the monkey mind, but doing so is not an end in itself. Techniques may help, but true worship begins where technique ceases.[114]

Historically and currently, Quakerism provides little guidance for what to do in silent worship because Quakers consider the Spirit the proper guide. However, Brinton suggests guidance may be helpful, and he turns to Catholic meditative tradition, with its four stages of prayer. The first is mental prayer, built on human imagination. One might mentally recreate a scene from the Gospels and reflect on it. Second is affective prayer, based mostly on feeling, perhaps empathy with Christ on the cross. Third is acquired contemplation, the willed emptying of the monkey mind. Fourth, infused contemplation occurs, which flows from God's initiative and is God's work.[115] However, Fox and Barclay clearly consider only the fourth stage true worship. According to the original Quaker vision, true worship abandons human imagination and will for worship that flows from the divine Light within.

Moreover, Fox does instruct the worshiper. He describes a method with distinct steps. First, turn inward; second, sit in the Light; third, see your sins; fourth, behold your savior; fifth live in the Light, mature in it.[116] The Light, says Fox, teaches us to know God and, through a kind of life-review, shows us our sins, then reveals our salvation and brings us peace.[117]

The Quaker way of worship is biblical. Fox claims Jesus himself initiated it when Jesus said, "Where two or three are gathered in my name, I am there among them" (Matt. 18:20).[118] Barclay observes Jesus left no directive in the Gospels about worship except the injunction to worship in the Spirit, and the whole New Testament contains only the instruction to meet together. Although Barclay knows the New Testament mentions that the followers of Jesus pray, preach, and sing, it does not prescribe an order for these activities, nor does it say they should begin immediately when Christians meet for worship.[119] However, the Bible often declares we should wait on God, watch before God, and be still. Barclay lists twenty-three instances, eleven from the Hebrew Scriptures and twelve from the New Testament.[120]

Gwyn notes that the Quaker way of worship resembles the worship described in 1 Corinthians 14 more closely than any other form of modern Christian worship does.[121] Here Paul tells the Corinthians to seek spiritual gifts, and especially prophecy, for prophets speak words of strength, encouragement, and consolation. (To prophesy does not mean to predict the future. Rather, it consists in reporting thoughts or words speakers believe come to them directly from God. Modern Quakers who give messages in Meeting are prophesying.) He then instructs them that, when they gather, one may offer a hymn, another a lesson, another a revelation, another a tongue, or an interpretation of what is spoken in tongues. But everything should be done to strengthen the group. Anyone speaking in a tongue should either have an interpreter or remain silent. Two or three might prophesy; the others should listen, consider what is said, and learn from it. Speak one at a time. And, finally, do everything "decently and in order," (14:40) for God is a God of peace, not of chaos.

Interestingly, modern charismatics constitute the other group claiming 1 Corinthians 14 for itself. Charismatics sing hymns, read lessons, prophesy, speak in tongues, and interpret. However, the Pauline passage does not mention a designated leader or a planned liturgy, whereas most charismatic churches have both. Modern Quakers who worship in the original manner have neither. However, they do not speak in tongues in Meeting, as far as I know. Therefore, no Christian denomination today has all the Pauline characteristics and only those, but Quakers do seem to come closest.

Carole Spencer makes the salient point that "No Christian tradition, outside of monasticism, had elevated the use of silence on a regular, communal basis to the extent of the early Quakers." She says Quakers employ silence as a symbol for the spiritual world to replace the symbols of most Christian liturgies, which can turn into idols that hide God's presence instead of mediating it.[122]

Barclay notes that Catholic mystics write of turning inward, repenting, and being led by the Spirit. Mature mystics conclude outward observances are useless. They even hinder communication from God. Therefore, Barclay says, the most saintly Christians in all ages agree that the supreme approach to God is to eliminate outward symbols and turn inward. The difference between Quakers and Catholics, he observes, is that Quakers think everyone should do this, not only the monastics.[123] Brinton adds that total withdrawal from the world as in monasticism is not for Quakers. Like monastics, Quakers experience God and consider the experience valuable in itself, but then they return to the world to be God's agents in creation and redemption, working with God to incarnate divinity in the world.[124]

The Quakers differ from the monastics in another way, too. Whereas monastics maintain silence and have individual spiritual directors to instruct them outside the context of worship, Quakers allow vocal ministry in their Meetings for Worship, the group together receives instruction, and any person worshiping within it may address it.

Vocal ministry for everyone

Logically, if everyone has the Light within, then all should be allowed, and even encouraged, to speak to the gathered Meeting, when they believe the Spirit has something to say to others through them. Men and women, black and white, Christian and non-Christian, even children, should be allowed to speak. This does not imply that everyone will speak. The early Quakers thought some especially gifted in this respect, as others were gifted in other respects. Nevertheless, no persons should be refused the opportunity as long as they speak "decently and in order," in St. Paul's words. Paul, too, believes any believer can receive a revelation.[125]

For the early Quakers, the question of whether women should speak in Meeting is a live one. Fox repeats his argument that Quakers are in the same state as Adam and Eve before the Fall. There, he says, Eve is a helpmate to Adam, not a subordinate. She, too, carries the Light within. Therefore, all in Meeting for Worship should heed women speakers as well as men speakers.[126] However eventually, Fox hopes outward teaching will become unnecessary, for the inner Teacher is sufficient.[127]

Barclay's reasons are more direct. "Since male and female are one in Christ Jesus [Gal. 3:28], and he gives his Spirit no less to one than to the other, we do not consider it in any way unlawful for a woman to preach in the assemblies of God's people when God so moves her by his Spirit."[128] He thinks the comments about not allowing women to speak in church (1 Cor. 14:33b-36) refer only to "inconsiderate and talkative women who caused trouble in the church."[129] Modern biblical critics think the passage a later interpolation. Although he lacks contemporary critical tools, Barclay often displays a modern sensitivity to biblical texts.

Unlike the preaching of other Christians around them, the early Quakers' preaching is nondoctrinal. They are not trying to lead people to a set of beliefs. Rather, they intend to help others experience the Light for themselves. Doctrine without experience is empty, they think.[130] Once people experience the Light within them, it will become their Teacher. This attitude continues at least through the nineteenth century. A Quaker convert, Caroline Stephen, in her lovely book on Quaker worship, warns against acquiring Quaker convictions second-hand.[131]

In a confrontation between Fox and an ordained minister, the minister offers to pray for Fox and asks Fox to pray for him, adding that he will give Fox the words with which to pray. Fox replies that he might as well use the set prayers in the Book of Common Prayer, but to do so would be to reject the early Christians' practice of praying through the Spirit.[132] Prayer by individuals alone and vocal prayer in Meeting for Worship are to be spontaneous, the voice of the Spirit, not formal, set prayers human beings create.

Stephen describes the vocal ministry in Meeting for Worship as "part-singing" to contrast it with singing in unison. She writes of the harmony of it, how the individual messages often fit together in oblique but concordant ways.[133]

Brinton judges the highest form of vocal ministry to be prayer, using the first person plural rather than singular.[134] He goes on to comment that the early church considered prophecy extremely important (1 Cor. 12:28; 14:1), but priests soon replaced prophets and turned prophecy into heresy. He thinks the change occurred because the church began to emphasize correct doctrine and high sacramentalism that required special persons set aside for the purpose, and he notes that Quakerism has neither,[135] and therefore prophecy should blossom in Quakerism today, as it did among the early Quakers.

For the early church, the gathered faithful constitute the body of Christ. Paul extends the metaphor to write of some being feet, ears, or eyes (1 Cor. 12). Metaphorically, these are the separate but necessary gifts and talents each brings so the body can function effectively. To refuse to contribute one's gift to the assembly is the equivalent of quenching the Spirit.[136] Paul understands all Christians as charismatics who share the Spirit.[137] Moreover, the gifts wander from person to person. One person might exercise a gift one day, another might display it the next. Therefore, the church had no fixed offices. Teaching, the conveying of tradition, came closest to being an office. Nonetheless, to interpret tradition required the Spirit.[138] In their practice of vocal ministry and lack of offices, the early Quakers recreate the early church as described in the New Testament. This is their intention.

Barclay says little about the purpose of vocal ministry. Probably, he thinks it obvious. Certainly, he is more concerned with those aspects of worship opponents criticized more often, like Quaker silence or lack of clergy, sacraments, and liturgy. However, he mentions that Quaker Meetings for Worship rarely pass in complete silence. Rather, the Spirit moves the gathered people to vocal exhortation and instruction of one another, and to prayer and praise of God.[139] Given this list, he probably thinks vocal ministry should consist of exhortation, instruction, prayer, and praise. These allow enormous latitude to the vocal minister.

The Quakers follow simple logic in not having a separate clergy. If everyone has the Light, why should only one person preach or prophesy? Nonetheless, the early Quakers offer other reasons for not having separate clergy. As a philosopher myself, I especially like one of Barclay's reasons. He notes that formal training in logic and philosophy lead the learned to develop inane and convoluted arguments and adds, "If you want to make a man a useless fool, teach him logic and philosophy. Before that, he may have been fit for something, but after it he will be good for nothing but speaking nonsense."[140] This from the learned Barclay! He goes on to condemn scholastic theology as "a paganization of the literal external knowledge of Christ. It is man in his fallen state. . . . serpentine and worldly wisdom."[141] Truth, he finds, is more likely to spring from an honest heart.[142] True knowledge of God comes from the Spirit. The person who has it need not hold credentials the learned institute. Indeed, the learned and credentialed should remain silent if they cannot speak from the Spirit. Instead, they should listen to those who speak from the Spirit, even if the speaker is illiterate.[143]

He also develops arguments based on the Bible. The law in the Hebrew Scriptures, he notes, makes priesthood hereditary, and Christianity derives the doctrine of apostolic succession from the law. (Apostolic succession claims the ministry of the church originates in the apostles and continues its legitimacy only through an unbroken line of consecrated bishops.) Christ, however, rejected such external relationships, Barclay claims.[144] Therefore, Christianity should reject them. Early Quakerism does.

Barclay also refers to the Bible when arguing that ministers should be unpaid. In Barclay's time, the Church of England was established by law, and everyone was tithed to pay the clergy. The Quakers refused to pay the tithe, and the law confiscated their goods and/or jailed them. Barclay argues that Christian ministers are not the Levitical priests of the Hebrew Scriptures. In the scriptures, the land belongs to twelve tribes, but the priestly tribe, called Levites, does not receive any land. Instead, they have a right to a tenth of the produce of the land, a tithe. However, the Bible grants ministers in England no such right.[145]

He also develops a moral argument, observing that the present practice of payment of clergy leads to greed, idleness, luxury, and worldliness among clergy, both Protestant and Catholic. The scandals have become so common they are proverbial.[146] Presumably, Barclay thinks unpaid clergy would be neither worldly nor profligate. Fox concurs. He adduces arguments from the Bible to demonstrate that paid clergy resemble the biblical priests the prophets castigate and also resemble the Pharisees, scribes, and priests Jesus condemns.[147]

Stephen, writing late in the nineteenth century, finds the unpaid Quaker ministry remains attractive. She commends it as free in three respects: open to all, spontaneous, and unpaid.[148] Today, Quaker ministers travel less than they did during the first three centuries, but the unpaid, vocal ministry in Meetings for Worship is a flourishing Quaker tradition.

Not having a paid clergy set aside for special functions is consistent with the early Quakers' elimination of outward sacraments.

The inner sacraments

Sacramental theology is complex. Here it is simplified. The majority of Christian traditions believe sacraments convey God's grace to the recipients if they place no impediments in the way, such as receiving communion without repenting their sins. Although the water of baptism and the bread and wine of Eucharistic communion are symbols, they are also thought to be vehicles, conveying grace to the recipients that affects the recipients inwardly.[149]

The Quakers believe all people have divine Light (God's grace) within themselves at all times. The goal is not to convey God's grace to people, but to awaken them to its inner presence. Therefore, external vehicles are not required to transport grace within. Logically, then, if people experience the Light within, they receive baptism of the Spirit and communion with God without requiring external symbols or vehicles. The early Quaker response to this logic is to eliminate the symbols, and yet to consider every Meeting for Worship sacramental, with the sacraments being celebrated internally. And, of course, if there are no special sacraments, no special clergy are required to consecrate the elements.

The Quakers are in saintly company. Through experience, the mystics, too, find turning inward, undergoing purgation of iniquity, and being drawn toward the Spirit make outward observances useless, even obstacles to the spiritual life. Possibly, outward symbols become idols, replacing the reality that is God and then being worshiped themselves rather than leading people beyond them to experience the divine. The tendency to turn symbols into idols is especially a danger with the Eucharistic bread in Catholicism, for Catholicism believes it becomes the actual body of Christ, and reserves it, lifts it up, and carries it in procession.

Moreover, mystical experience sees God permeate everything. For the mystic and the early Quakers, God is present everywhere, so all things become sacramental, just as all days are holy for the early Quakers.

Living in an age before science and biblical criticism rendered the authority of the Bible suspect or illusory, the early Quakers expended much energy trying to prove the sacraments unbiblical rather than arguing logically for their elimination. This approach made sense because arguing logically from Quaker first principles for their elimination would not have convinced opponents unless the opponents accepted the principles, and most did not, whereas all accepted the authority of the Bible.

Thus, Barclay begins his argument against his opponents by observing that the term *sacrament* is not in the Bible.[150] Literally, he is correct. It never appears in the King James Version, the standard English translation of Barclay's time. However, the original New Testament is in Greek. Jerome translated it into Latin for the Catholic Church toward the end of the fourth century, and the Latin version became the official one. The English term *sacrament* comes from the Latin term *sacramentum,* which translates the Greek *mysterion,* mystery in English. *Mysterion* changes from meaning a secret in the Greek translation of biblical book of Daniel and intertestamental works to meaning a secret symbol by the middle of the second century C.E. In the fourth century, the Latin *sacramentum* must have meant the same thing. *Mysterion* occurs in the original Greek of Matthew, Mark, Luke, six of the epistles, and Revelation.[151] Barclay knows the languages. The English of the King James Version, published in 1611, retains the Greek derivation, translating *mysterion* as mystery rather than sacrament. Admittedly, however, *mysterion* in the New Testament does not refer to sacraments as Barclay knows them. The doctrine familiar to Barclay developed only with scholastic theology from the end of the eleventh century.[152] Nonetheless, Barclay's claim that the term *sacrament* is not in the Bible is somewhat disingenuous.

In a second argument, Barclay claims Protestants and Catholics are Judaizers because they depend on outward ceremonies, just as the Jews did in the Temple. In contrast, Barclay says, the new covenant is spiritual and inward, written on the heart.[153] Catholics and Protestants retain the form, he declares, while denying the power of God.[154] Barclay thinks we are living in a different dispensation from that recorded in the Hebrew Scriptures. Then, God required rites and ceremonies to counter the Jews' tendency toward idolatry. Now, in the new dispensation, only meeting together is necessary.[155]

Having dispensed with sacraments in general, Barclay turns to the two sacraments common to Catholic and Protestant, baptism and Eucharist. There is one baptism, writes Barclay, quoting Ephesians 4:5. It is pure and spiritual (Gal. 3:27), Barclay says, "the baptism of the Spirit and of fire" that washes and purges us from our sins. John the Baptist's water baptism was temporary (John 3:30), and infant baptism is unscriptural, a human invention.[156]

Jesus, Barclay notes, did not command water baptism.[157]
Moreover, Paul declares he was not sent to baptize, so the gospel
he knew cannot have commanded water baptism.[158] Furthermore,
Jesus left no instructions about worship, except that it is spiritual.[159]

Modern scholars agree. John Meier, a respected New
Testament scholar, comments that John's baptism foreshadows as
symbol the outpouring of the Spirit the prophets had foreseen;
John's baptism is a symbol anticipating God's forgiveness that will
actually occur only at the last judgment.[160] Jaroslav Pelikan, in his
history of Christian doctrine, notes that the early church Fathers
considered baptism inefficacious unless the Holy Spirit cleansed
the sins of the baptized and sanctified them.[161]

Barclay wrestles ineffectively with the commission Matthew
attributes to the risen Jesus to baptize all "in the name of the Father
and of the Son and of the Holy Spirit" (28:19), but modern scholarship rescues him. Neither the formula nor the commission are
from Jesus, but products of the early church. Moreover, the commission is Matthew's individual vision for the early church. It fits
well neither with Mark's nor Luke's vision.[162]

On the Eucharist, Barclay grants considerable agreement
between the Quakers and their opponents. All agree, he says, that
the body and blood of Christ are necessary to nourish the soul, and
the souls of believers do, in fact, feed upon them.[163] Everyone also
agrees that people commune by soul and spirit.[164] But here, agreement ends. The bread and wine of communion, Barclay observes,
are physical. They cannot feed the soul and spirit.[165]

In considering the Eucharist, Barclay claims Protestants and
Catholics make two major errors. First, they relate the body of the
historical Jesus who walked and suffered in Galilee and Judea to
the spiritual, divine Light that nourishes people in all ages. Second,
they relate the meal ceremony of Jesus and his disciples to the body
and blood of Christ.[166] However, Barclay notes, Jesus often used
everyday objects as metaphors to teach spiritual lessons.[167]
Similarly, he used the bread and wine as metaphors to raise the disciples' minds to spiritual things.[168] He was not being literal.
Communion, Barclay claims, is a mystery hidden from the unspir-
itual. The body and blood are celestial, with no earthly elements.
In contrast, the bread and wine are earthly. People receive them
and yet remain spiritually empty. Real communion is inward and

spiritual. Outward elements are not required. Communion occurs whenever people experience the Light within and enjoy its nourishment, which may happen any time, but especially in Quaker Meeting for Worship.[169]

Yet, Barclay concedes, some in receiving the Eucharistic elements experience the Holy Spirit at work in themselves. From this experience, they mistakenly derive the doctrines of transubstantiation and consubstantiation. (These are Catholic and Lutheran doctrines respectively. Both declare Jesus' real body and blood are present after the elements are consecrated.) The Holy Spirit is at work in some recipients, Barclay agrees, but the bread and wine are not the cause.[170]

Although modern scholars disagree among themselves about the exact meaning of the Eucharist, they have dismantled the biblical passages on which Christian doctrines rest. Partly this has occurred because modern scholarship has concluded that the Gospels have two separable strands: sayings and events that go back to the historical Jesus and those the early church created. Cooper notes that the Gospels record the command, "Do this in remembrance of me" only in Luke 22:19-20 [actually 19b], but the command is not in the earliest extant manuscripts. Thus, he decides the command does not go back to Jesus (or even to Luke's Gospel, composed some fifty years after Jesus' death) but is a creation of the early church.[171]

The Jesus Seminar, consisting of some two hundred New Testament scholars meeting over a period of years to consider the authenticity of each saying attributed to Jesus, concludes that the words attributed to Jesus at the Last Supper differ so much from one Gospel to another, (and again in 1 Corinthians 11:23-26) they can never be recovered.[172] One of the giants of historical Jesus scholarship thinks Jesus did not institute a Last Supper, the final supper was not a Passover meal and therefore had no passion symbolism, and Paul's body and blood language are martyrological rather than sacramental, which is why Paul says the celebration "proclaims the Lord's *death*."[173] Pelikan notes that the doctrine of the real presence of the body and blood of Christ in the Eucharist was not formulated until the ninth century.[174] And Bruce Chilton, another scholar of the historical Jesus, argues that Jesus turned the plant-derived bread and wine of his meals into symbols to substitute metaphorically for the blood sacrifice of the Temple, of which

Jesus disapproved.[175] After studying the subject, I reached the same conclusion.[176]

Fox, perhaps, speaks the last and most vivid word. Arguing with a Jesuit who believes the Catholic doctrine that the bread and wine are Christ, and thus immortal and divine, Fox offers a test. Take a bottle of wine and a loaf of bread, he suggests, and divide them in half. Let priests consecrate whichever half they choose, then put the consecrated and unconsecrated bread and wine into a cellar with seven locks and seven watchers. If the consecrated bread and wine do not grow moldy and sour, Quakers will turn Catholic; if they do, Catholics will turn Quaker. Awkwardly, the Jesuit wriggles out of the contest![177]

This chapter has argued that the appropriateness of silent Quaker Meeting for Worship follows logically from the core principles of the early Quakerism. Logically, those adopting Quaker theology should worship in silence, without sacraments or separated clergy, but with vocal ministry possible for all. Moreover, Barclay's arguments combined with modern biblical scholarship demonstrate that the Quaker way of worship is biblical, whereas the Bible does not command worship with outward liturgy or sacraments. The Quaker method of reaching decisions together is biblical and logical, too.

4. DECISIONS: UNITING IN THE LIGHT

QUAKERS ORGANIZE their practical affairs and frame decisions for their community in assemblies known formally as Meeting for Worship for Business or, more briefly but less accurately, Meeting for Business. While Quakers in Meeting for Worship seek communion with God and long to absorb the Light, those same Quakers in Meeting for Business seek God's will.[178] Both Meetings appeal to the collective as well as the individual. As those in Meeting for Worship concentrate on their own inner states, but also expect to reflect the Light in others, so those in Meeting for Business speak as individuals while seeking practical ways to express God's will for the group.[179]

Barclay's *Apology* hardly mentions Quaker organization, probably because he addressed that subject two years earlier in his *Anarchy of the Ranters* (1674), a judicious statement of Fox's thoughts on Quaker organization.[180] Because the *Anarchy* is available only as a facsimile of the original seventeenth century text, with all its peculiarities of punctuation and spelling, there are no direct quotations from it here, but paraphrases, employing the same techniques of modernization used for other seventeenth century works. This chapter, then, uses several works, including Barclay's *Anarchy*, to discuss the philosophy and practice of early Quaker group decision-making. It also asks how Quakers think they know they are following the Light rather than their own egos.

In some ways, the philosophy behind Quaker group decisions is simple. Because the Light within is single, those living in its glow have faith they will arrive at unity.

Unity in the Light

According to Barclay, when controversies arise among Quakers, the Holy Spirit decides the issue, and the Spirit is infallible. That

35

the Spirit decides, Barclay says, sets the Quakers apart from all other groups claiming to be Christian.[181] The Catholic Church, he notes, places infallibility in outer offices, places, or stations, and then excommunicates and/or persecutes those who question the Church's authority.[182] Protestants convene councils of clergy and elders, vote, and then require everyone to receive their decisions as authoritative.[183] In contrast, the Quakers decline to exclude members, refuse to persecute dissenters, and eschew the vote.[184] Instead, they listen for the judgment of the Spirit delivered through the sanctified and submit to the decision because it comes from God, and God is true.[185]

Quakers know the problem of authority is never solved by passing authority to another. Caroline Stephen notes that authority necessarily springs from within those deciding. If we choose to give our authority to another, we ourselves, nonetheless, have exercised our choice.[186] We cannot escape responsibility for our decisions. We can only hope we make them from a divine center rather than an egocentric position. Quakers do not have authorities. However, they do recognize that some Quakers carry more weight than others do. They even call them "weighty Quakers." Other terms are Biblical – elders and overseers. They also form committees, commonly called "clearness committees" to try to help people facing decisions decide whether they are see the way clear to continue on the path they are considering. So, Quakers are realistic and help one another.

Fox's intention was to reconstitute the authority and decision-practices of the early church. In disputes with Protestants, he argues that Protestant practices differ from those of Christ and the apostles, adding, "'If you have not the same power and spirit, then it is manifest that you are led by another power and spirit than the apostles and Church in the primitive times.'"[187] He notes that while other professing Christians think Matthew, Mark, Luke, and John provide the Gospel, he proclaims "The Gospel was the power of God, which was preached before Matthew, Mark, Luke and John . . . were printed or written, and was preached to every creature who might never see nor hear of the four books aforesaid."[188] This one, single power of God, this Spirit, this Light, exists from the beginning, empowers the early church, and consolidates it. It constitutes the only head and unifier of the church.

Without benefit of modern scholarship, Fox accurately perceives the role and authority of the Spirit in the early church. James

Dunn notes that the word *koinonia* appears first in the New Testament after Luke's account of Pentecost (Acts 2). *Koinonia* means community, fellowship, of one mind. The one, single Spirit produces a united community, with the risen Christ at its head, leading and commissioning people in resurrection appearances and visions, providing authority and power. Dunn summarizes his study of the early Christian sense of community by commenting that it springs from the common experience of the Holy Spirit, the Pentecost experience. It is not found in hierarchy, tradition, liturgy, sacrament, or even in the resurrection appearances, but in charismatic worship.[189]

Later, Dunn contrasts Jesus' community with that of the early church. Jesus calls disciples, whereas Paul forms a charismatic fellowship. The disciples rely on Jesus for teaching and prophecy, but Paul's community depends on one another. While Jesus lived, he provided authority, yet for Paul's community authority descends from God through everyone, and the whole community together exercises authority. Jesus' disciples exist for mission, Paul's community for mission, surely, but also for building itself up, creating a charismatic fellowship. Dunn ends the contrast by noting that, for Paul, "only a charismatic community functioning as such could hope to manifest adequately the same grace that God manifested in the one man Jesus."[190] Certainly, Fox would agree, and he creates a similar community, held together in love by the one Spirit, by traveling ministers, and by letters, Paul's own techniques for consolidation.

Dunn finishes his study by noting that in the first and second generation of Christians – and now! – four corporate responses to the Christ-event are possible. Luke exemplifies the first. He rejoices in charismatic experiences while ignoring the problems they raise. Paul represents the second. He forms one charismatic community led by the one Spirit. The Pastoral Epistles to Timothy and Titus epitomize the third. They quench the Spirit in favor of tradition. John embodies the fourth. He rejects institutions and sacraments and emphasizes a direct relationship with Jesus in the present, similar to the relationship the disciples experienced when Jesus was with them.[191]

According to Dunn's scheme, Fox follows Paul and John. He rejects institutions and sacraments and attempts to form a unified, charismatic community. However, he is aware of the problems, and one of his answers to the danger of anarchy is to form Quaker Meetings for Worship for Business dependent on the Spirit of Christ for communal leadership. Because Fox usually conflates the historical Jesus, the risen Christ, the power of God, the Gospel, and the Light, he is not concerned with whether his communities form a relationship with Christ, the Spirit, or the Light – or any of a dozen other metaphors for charismatic experiences. He thinks they will come to unity because they follow a single Spirit.

Fox invents a term for his organizing effort, the *Gospel order*. For Fox, the Gospel is the power of God. Thus, the Gospel order is not a method for organizing found in the Gospels, but order that springs from God, from the charismatic Spirit. It comes from the Light within rather than from external authority[192] of any sort, including the scriptures. It is the power of God to bring order and harmony to the community.[193]

Fox has faith that unity will come if his community is sufficiently patient and attentive to the Light because the Light is single. When asked what a church is, Fox answers, "I told him the Church was the pillar and ground of Truth, made up of living stones, living members, a spiritual household which Christ was the head of, but he was not the head of a mixed multitude, or of an old house made up of lime, stones, and wood."[194] Fox is adamant. During a sermon that in retrospect marks the beginning of Quakerism, Fox says Christ has come to England, he is here now, Christ "who ended the temple, and the priests, and the tithes, and Christ said, 'Learn of me.'" Fox thinks God has sent him "so that they [who are erring] might all come to know Christ their teacher, their counsellor, their shepherd to feed them, and their bishop to oversee them and their prophet to open to them, and to know their bodies to be the temples of God and Christ for them to dwell in."[195] Fox never strays from this position. His calling is to lead others to their inner Teacher, Christ, who will teach them himself. Fox is not their teacher. He refuses all offers of preaching positions.

Barclay repeats Fox's claim that people are living in the Gospel dispensation, with various persons having diverse tasks and talents,[196] but all guided by one Spirit. Ambler, in his comments on Fox, notes that the early Quakers lived in unity and peace because the Light is single. There is but one reality, one truth.[197]

Yet, the unity the early Quakers experienced was not outward conformity or agreement on a common creed or covenant. Isaac Penington, Fox's contemporary, says the Quakers form a fellowship that meets in the Light, not an assembly that agrees with each other. Unity is preserved by staying in the Light, not by conformity.[198] Paul Lacey, writing in this century, concurs. He thinks mutual agreement might be satisfying, but it does not imply obedience to the Spirit.[199]

One way to have unity without conformity is to distinguish substantial matters from those that change with culture and time, like the requirement for circumcision, says Barclay.[200] In his modern study of Quaker decision-making, Michael Sheeran agrees. He notes that the community needs conformity on fundamentals, but on secondary matters, there can be unity without uniformity.[201] Today, it is possible to have a Quaker Meeting where all agree that silent worship, mutual respect, and love are central and enriching, yet agree on little else.

The main difficulty with depending on the Light for unity and fellowship is the tension between individual inspiration and Spirit-led group decision-making. Barclay notes that there needs to be a balance between the inner experience of the individual, who may prophesy, and the authority of the group, also based on prophecy. All must be done for edification and not destruction.[202] As 1 Corinthians 14:32-3 (Barclay's source) says, "The spirits of the prophets are subject to the prophets, for God is a God not of disorder but of peace." Douglas Gwyn, in his book on Fox, puts it nicely. If God is a father, he says, then the Quaker church is the mother, and the children of the Light are to mature under the authority of both heavenly parents.[203]

However, Sheeran comments that such a balance, with its strong sense of community, is difficult to maintain in today's society, which praises individualism and encourages selfishness. He asks how Quakers can maintain community today and offers three methods. The first is to withdraw from the larger society, as the Mennonites have done, but that is not the Quaker way. Second, Quakers might educate their children to be different and, third, Quakers might emphasize religious experience.[204] Certainly, Fox and Barclay would commend the third way, for religious experience forms the center of their lives. Nonetheless, they would not object to the second, for Quakers in the seventeenth century differed from their contemporaries. Yet, I think they would stress that Quaker difference must stem from heeding the Light within, not from calculated external nonconformity.

So, this is the early Quaker philosophy of a united community. Because the Light within is single, those enlightened become one. Moreover, to keep individuals from straying, who falsely believe the Light is leading them when their own egos are in control, the group can censure individual behavior for failing to conform to the righteousness of the Light. Yet, unity of belief is not required. The central requirement is fellowship in love that springs from the Light within. Although the philosophy is abstract, the early Quakers knew how to practice unity.

Unity in practice

The purposes of Meeting for Worship for Business are practical. Fox devises them under persecution, when the arrested need legal advice, children require care while their parents are in prison, and those ruined by fines seek financial aid. Moreover, Fox is always concerned for the destitute, feels compassion for them, hands them his own money, and collects money from the Meetings to offer them.[205] He establishes schools where Quaker children can learn practical subjects and helps them get apprenticeships so they can earn their own livings and not become beggars.

Because the earliest Quakers worship in homes, barns, and fields, they do not have collective bills to pay, but before Fox's death, they acquire buildings as places for worship and assembly and, so, also accumulated bills. Today, Meetings for Business oversee finances, worship, education, marriages, funerals, libraries, buildings, camps, and schools, and every Meeting does something for the community, often working for peace or in prisons or for poor relief. Yet, they have no leader but the Spirit.

Quaker organization can be confusing. Meetings are named for the frequency of their business meetings. Hence, although it worships at least weekly, the local Meeting is called the Monthly Meeting because it holds Meeting for Business once a month. Quarterly Meetings consist of an assembly of perhaps a dozen Monthly Meetings that meet for business four times a year. Yearly Meetings are composed of a larger number of Quarterly Meetings that meet together for business once a year, generally for a week and often today on university campuses, where expenses are minimized. The Yearly Meetings are comparable to a diocese, since they are composed of Meetings in a specific geographical area. However, they are dioceses without hierarchy, and power flows from the bottom up. Nonetheless, they perform some of the same functions dioceses do.

Every Meeting for Business has a clerk. Originally, the clerk functioned as a clerk or secretary to record the Meeting's decisions. Today, the idea is maintained, although in practice the clerk presides,[206] and a separate person keeps records. Nonetheless, the clerk does not lead, but encourages others to speak and tries to ascertain the sense of the Meeting, to feel the Spirit's movement through God's gathered people. This means the clerk must have the ability to interpret the sense of the Meeting,[207] for no votes are taken. This is a special skill, partly of listening well, partly of spiritual sensitivity. Unfortunately, there is no guarantee that persons so blessed will also have other necessary skills, like being organized.[208] Nonetheless, being organized will not make a good clerk if spiritual sensitivity is lacking. This need for spirituality, plus some contemporary Quakers' strong mistrust of leadership of any sort,[209] makes the clerkship a complex, but rewarding, calling.

Perhaps the most outstanding aspect of Meeting for Business is its atmosphere, which one word describes, respect. Quakers respect one another. They are also open to each other and are unusually humble. Being non-violent, they do not shout each other down or indulge in sarcastic remarks. In part, their respect for each other arises because of their common belief that everyone has the Light within. In part, it comes because Quakers are wary of claiming truth for themselves, although they are willing to acknowledge their small piece of it. Moreover, they enter Meeting for Business with the belief that all are seeking the best solution to whatever problems confront them and that the group can arrive at a best solution through worshiping and working together. They do not come to promote their own pet agendas. Hence, they do not vote because voting fails to respect the minority. Nor do they compromise because compromises tend to the lowest common denominator. Instead, the goal is to achieve a synthesis, to agree upward, as Brinton puts it.[210] A metaphor may help. Meeting for Business is like an orchestra. All have their notes to contribute. If one person fails to contribute, the piece is incomplete, but if one person tries to be the whole, the harmony is destroyed. And always, there is an atmosphere of respect.[211]

Visitors inattentive to atmosphere could recognize a Quaker Meeting for Business by its other characteristics. The apparent leader does not lead. No one votes. All participate on a basis of equality. Deliberate periods of silence occur that might seem lengthy. Members work together toward solutions without compromise. The goal is to find the will of God, which may transcend every initial position. This is what the members want, for God has touched them, they have sat in the Light.[212]

Moreover, Quakers welcome differences. Variety of opinion promotes growth, providing a way to agree upward.[213] Quakers can be as diverse as they are because they emphasize the experience of the gathered Meeting, sitting in the Light. The experience demands decrease of self-interest and pursuit of a truth that exceeds any one individual. In important matters in Meeting for Business, extended silences allow individuals to reenter this experience and find a higher solution,[214] perhaps a solution no one initially considered.

Sometimes, Meeting for Business faces difficulties that divide it. Quakers recognize three degrees of dissent. First, someone may disagree, but not stand in the way. If this occurs, the Meeting records its decision and proceeds to act. Second, a dissenter might say, "Minute me as opposed." Then the record of the Meeting will state this person's opposition, by name, but still stand by its decision and act on it. This is unusual, but represents a stronger dissent than the first. Finally, the Meeting may fail to come to unity, in which case the clerk will delay the decision to a future Meeting, when all will have had time to reconsider their positions.[215]

In exploring the decision-process of Quaker Meeting for Business, Sheeran discovers the Quaker way of making decisions works for them because all believe in a force for unity that guides the Meeting, and that force is in everyone, so everyone deserves respect and equal treatment.[216] The force is the infallible Light.

The infallible Light

Because the early Quakers consider the Light divine, they deem it true, infallibly so. Yet, infallibility does not reside in offices, places, or special persons, as in Catholicism, or in councils, votes, confessions, and covenants, as in Protestantism. Nor is it found in the scriptures, although it is their source. No one can interpret the scriptures correctly unless the Light inspires the interpreter. In addition, finally, the Light shines within and through human beings, themselves fallible.

I think Stephen understands the Light well when she writes of it as a Spirit of truth, but not omniscient. Rather, in us it is a Spirit of truth in thought, word, and deed, a Spirit that creates and promotes integrity. It does not offer intellectual knowledge, but purification, not ecstasy, but holiness. She thinks the Quakers correctly emphasize moral and spiritual righteousness rather than doctrinal rightness. Perhaps we can never reach doctrinal truth, statements that encapsulate God, but we can partake of Truth, of Spirit, of Christ, of God's power and presence.[217]

Nonetheless, discernment is a perennial problem for people claiming spiritual enlightenment. Are there any signs or tests enabling the people themselves or, better yet, objective observers, to know they are spiritually inspired rather than egocentrically self-deceived or even demon-driven?

The central answer for the early Quakers is biblical. Matthew and Luke have John the Baptist (Matt. 3:8; Luke 3:8) and Jesus (Matt. 7:15-20; 12:33-37; Luke 6:43-45) say we can recognize good and evil people by their fruits. Matthew applies the idea specifically to false prophets (Matt. 7:15). Paul expresses the same thought in Galatians 5:16-26 where he contrasts works of the flesh with works of the Spirit. Unlike the Gospel writers, he lists examples. Works of the flesh include fornication, impurity, licentiousness, strife, jealousy, anger and envy, whereas works of the Spirit are love, joy, peace, patience, generosity, gentleness, and self-control.

Fox mentions obeying God and being righteous, holy, and honest in word and action.[218] Stephen comments that Quakers have always accepted the Bible as one standard and that "no claim to Divine inspiration could be justified except by the actual possession of the righteousness taught by Christ Himself in word and in deed."[219]

Sheeran mentions Paul's list, but also plain speech, inner silence, something that goes against one's wishes or natural will, and agreement of the community.[220] The latter would spring from

Paul's spirits of the prophets that are subject to the prophets, a call for communal agreement among those who prophesy.

And, yet, for the early Quakers scripture is not the primary guide. For Fox, the Gospel is the power of God, not the words of the New Testament.[221] Barclay writes, "In summary, if it is only by the Spirit that we can come to the true knowledge of God, and if it is by the Spirit that we are led into all truth and taught all things, then the Spirit – and not the scriptures – is the foundation and the basis of all truth and knowledge [of God and righteousness]."[222] Furthermore, he thinks the scriptures fail to provide an adequate guide to life. They contain insufficient instruction. For example, he says, God provides some with specific callings, but they cannot ascertain what their callings are by perusing scripture. God calls some to preach and some to serve, but scripture does not tell individuals which calling they have received, not to mention whether to preach or serve in England or France, Holland or Germany. Everyone also has a special role in the body of Christ, but scripture does not tell any whether to be a head or a foot, to use Paul's metaphor.[223]

Moreover, individuals have different gifts and talents that, in community, provide complementary roles or relationships.[224] As Paul notes, the gifts of the Spirit are distributed, but the Spirit is one (1 Cor. 12:4-31). Yet, scripture does not tell individuals what gifts they have. As Fox notes, the end of Christianity is holiness and the Church consists of those who are holy (1 Cor. 1:2),[225] but individuals are holy in different ways.

Therefore, to know whether anyone is following the Light is to seek signs of a righteous life. Yet, caution is required. Not everyone recognizes righteousness. Jesus, Fox, and the early Quakers aroused anger, hatred, and persecution. Gandhi and Martin Luther King, Jr., were assassinated. Today, former President Jimmy Carter's peacemaking efforts are ridiculed on late night television. Apparently, it takes inspiration by the Light to recognize righteousness in others.

Furthermore, although the Spirit may lead to righteous behavior, righteous behavior does not necessarily lead to the Spirit. People can refrain from doing anything on Paul's list – not drink, gamble, engage in frivolous games, or in sex outside marriage – yet lack the Spirit. Such behavior displays a pretended spirituality that amounts to lack of integrity. Often, the result is self-righteousness, pride in one's own ethical/spiritual accomplishments. As Fox would warn, these accomplishments spring from human nature, not from the Light within. Pretense, lack of integrity, and self-righteousness are the opposite of what Paul, Fox, and the early Quakers tried to engender. So, no signs are certain. Yet fruits, especially the Quaker convictions, known as testimonies as discussed in the next chapter, can constitute signs.

The problem of authority, of who and how the Spirit instructs, plagues the Quakers, as it has all Christian groups. Some answer with a strict top-down hierarchy, with an infallible man on top,[226] who makes mistakes. Others respond by claiming the scriptures infallible, but then fight over interpretations. Others create veritable anarchy. In their earliest days, the Quakers tended more toward anarchy than hierarchy – and they still do, but that first generation learned it needed guidance and developed Meetings for Business to transact the practical, daily affairs of the group and to call roaming individuals back to the holy fold. In the next century, Quaker elders gained considerable power and enforced strict Quaker behavior, but not doctrine.

Then came the nineteenth century. In 1827 in America, those who called themselves Quakers splintered into two groups (and, later, into more). Brinton says the main clash was between mysticism and evangelicalism, between the inner and the outer, that the elders tried to regulate theological thinking rather than only controlling behavior.[227] Whether the initial cause of the division was authoritarianism or doctrinal difference is unclear. One side claimed one, the other the other. Nonetheless, one side relied on the Light within much as the early Quakers had, whereas the other elevated scripture further than Fox or Barclay would have accepted. Brinton calls the rift "a theological controversy between the followers of the historic Christ and the followers of the Inward Christ,"[228] but this is not quite right. Indeed no Quaker author I have read has correctly understood the conceptual issues involved.

The early Quakers believed the Bible true, but in need of interpretation by the Spirit. They conflated the historical Jesus with the risen Christ, with the Light within, and believed the Light to be the primary authority, the Bible secondary. As a result, they knit together three separate concepts that later scholars disentangled.

The first concept only developed toward the end of the eighteenth century and became popular in the nineteenth and again in the late twentieth century. This is the concept of the historical Jesus, the man born in Nazareth and crucified outside Jerusalem, whom scholars can study apart from religious commitments. Anyone, Christian or not, can try to describe the man Jesus, his actions and teachings, using evidence in the New Testament along with various extrabiblical materials – textual, archaeological, and sociological – many discovered only in the last century.

The second concept is the Logos, the eternal Christ, the Spirit who enlightened people before Jesus was born, became incarnate in Jesus, and still shines within people today. This is the early Quakers' Christ, Gospel, Holy Spirit, and Light within, the divine, experiential, transforming power of God.

The third is Jesus Christ who died as a sacrifice for our sins, rose bodily from the grave, and ascended to heaven, to return someday in the future. When the early Quakers' opponents accuse them of denying the historical Christ or slighting history or the blood atonement, this is the concept they used. However, this is not history. This is doctrine. History says the Romans crucified Jesus outside the walls of Jerusalem in about 33 C.E. when Pilate ruled Judea. Doctrine declares why, theologically: he was crucified as a sacrifice for our sins. Doctrine also raises him from the dead and sends him to heaven. These doctrines cannot be proved from historical evidence. To be believed, they require faith commitment – and an outmoded cosmology.

The early Quakers fused these three concepts, one historical, one experiential, and one doctrinal. Scientific and scholarly discoveries of later times separated them, and the Quaker rift is only one consequence in Christianity of that fracturing.

The 1827 split occurs when one group of Quakers emphasizes the second concept, the Light, the centerpiece of early Quaker theology, whereas the second group exalts the third, the doctrine of Jesus' atoning sacrifice that the early Quakers' opponents accused them of slighting. The second group rejected the authority of the Light within to elevate literal scripture as interpreted through Protestant dogma. They departed from Fox's and Barclay's metaphorical reading of scripture. Barclay intended to refute Protestant literalism and dogmatism when he wrote his *Catechism*, based on scripture, and his *Apology,* founded on scripture and reason.

Therefore, it is both unhistorical and conceptually confused to declare that the Light within failed to maintain unity among the Quakers, as Fox and Barclay thought it would. On the contrary, one group of Quakers abandoned the divine and infallible Light as its primary authority and replaced it with scripture. Only when some Quakers deserted the Light did unity cease. Those Quakers who have continued to follow the Light remain in unity. Fox and Barclay knew from their personal experience of the English civil war that making scripture the primary authority causes division. They had faith that the Light within brings unity, if properly heeded. So far, their faith is well founded.

Today, concepts one and two, the historical Jesus and the Light within, mesh nicely, whereas concept three is untenable. Before delving into these issues, however, discussion of the original Quaker theology needs completion. One more subject remains, the Quakers' ideas about how to live daily life, ideas captured in the original Quaker testimonies.

5. TESTIMONIES: LIVING IN THE LIGHT

A TESTIMONY is what a witness tells in court, an affirmation of the facts, of the truth. For Quakers, truth is the Light within. The Light produces righteous lives and holy relationships. While Meeting for Worship longs for communion with the Light and Meeting for Worship for Business seeks the divine will for the Quaker community, the testimonies remind individuals and the community how to lead holy lives in public on a daily basis.

Cooper says the testimonies are "an outward sign of what Friends [Quakers] believe to be an inward revelation of truth." They resemble sacraments, he notes, for sacraments are also outward signs of inward grace. The testimonies spring from a concern for holiness, for alignment with the divine order. They are only secondarily rooted in a passion for social justice. At their center is the notion of integrity, harmony between beliefs and actions.[229]

Direct experience of God, Lacey comments, is insufficient for Quakers. They test their experiences through living daily by those experiences.[230] Acting on the testimonies provides visible witnesses to the Light within.

The testimonies spring from an enlightened conscience, the mutually enlightened consciences of the community of Quakers. Fox exhorts Quakers traveling in ministry,

> And this is the word of the Lord God to you all, and a charge to you all in the presence of the living God, be patterns, be examples, that your carriage and life may preach among all sorts of people, and to them. Then you will come to walk cheerfully over the world, answering that of God in every one.[231]

Fox's exhortation is explicitly to traveling ministers, but implicitly to all Quakers. They are to be examples to all people by their

48

way of life. However, Fox does not specify which actions are exemplary.

Barclay is more specific. He reminds his readers that Lucifer is the prince of this world[232] and that

> The chief purpose of all religion is to redeem men from the spirit and vain pursuits of this world, and to lead them into inward communion with God. All vain and empty customs and habits, whether of word or deed, should be rejected by those who have come to fear the Lord.[233]

Even though Quakers live in the world and are married and employed, their lives are as holy as cloistered lives are.[234] Because of the reputation for holy living Quakers have developed, others expect them to refrain from common behaviors such as indulging in extravagant language, being impatient or angry, or even laughing contemptuously. They expect them not only to keep their promises, but also to honor them assiduously. Quakers, Barclay notes, are known as a "pure and clean-living people."[235]

Many in the seventeenth century disapprove of the Quakers' way of worship, but their daily behavior provokes the most resentment. They refuse to take oaths, to address people by their titles, or to remove their hats in court. Those who expect to be treated with deference find such behavior insulting, become enraged, and persecute. Fox notes that often a thousand Quakers at once are in prison. Others are removed from office or ejected from the army.[236] The authorities confiscate their horses, cows, grain, and dinnerware, whip them, and put them in the stocks. The common people reprimand them and beat them.[237]

Barclay notes that, while other victimized groups meet in secret to worship after their own manner, the Quakers worship openly and resist persecution passively. As a result, the authorities find them uncontrollable. The authorities command a meeting to cease, but the Quakers remain, and then the authorities must remove all individually. Furthermore, they must then forcefully restrain them, or they return to the Meeting. The authorities destroy Meetinghouses, and Quakers meet in the rubble. The authorities arm themselves, yet the Quakers remain unafraid, and then those with arms realize they need to kill all there, and cannot, for their consciences bother them, so they leave without completing their intended task.[238]

This chapter is about the public, unvarying Quaker testimonies that drive both commoners and authorities to bewilderment and persecution in the seventeenth century. Today, many often admire similar behaviors, if curiously. Then and now, the Quaker testimonies spring, primarily, from enlightened consciences.

Conscience

As noted in an earlier chapter, Barclay thinks the human conscience is natural, not of divine creation. Culture forms and influences it and, therefore, it may constitute a poor guide to right and wrong. Nonetheless, he believes whoever acts against conscience sins, that acting contrary to conscience, even a wrong conscience resulting in a wrong action, is "absolutely unacceptable to God."[239]

This view was standard at the time and still is. Medieval scholars agreed that acting contrary to conscience is always sinful, whether the outcome is right or wrong, because the intent is to do wrong. They also agreed that culture influences conscience. Nonetheless, they believed nature enables people to grasp basic moral principles, derive moral precepts from them, and apply these to specific situations. Because these views were common, Barclay does not argue for them, but assumes his readers concur.

However, Barclay also differs from his predecessors, especially Thomas Aquinas, the central theologian of the Catholic Church. He believes no one should use force to try to alter someone else's conscience. God, he says, is the only suitable teacher and ruler of conscience.[240]

God refrains from force, but persuades, Barclay claims. The ideal conscience is one God enlightens through the Light within – a Light everyone possesses – until it conforms people to the divine image.

However, Barclay believes authorities may use force if life or property are threatened. Some people might argue that their conscience tells them to kill their neighbors, steal from them, or wreck their property. Use the law to restrain or punish them, counsels Barclay. No one should be free to do anything that would "prejudice the life or property of his neighbor, or do anything that is destructive to human society or inconsistent with its welfare. In such cases, the transgressor should be subject to the law."[241]

Barclay and Fox recognize civil authority, as did St. Paul (Rom. 13:1-7). Tension in Quakerism arises when Quakers occupy civil offices that may order violence, as happened in colonial Pennsylvania. Stephen thinks Quakers should not accept such offices.[242]

Although the state may use force to protect life and property, Barclay thinks it should not use force to impose the Church's policies,[243] as all state churches did at the time. Barclay argues that to use force against conscience contravenes the laws of reason and of nature. Torturing people fails to alter their minds, especially about divine matters. Minds can change, but only through sound reason and divine persuasion.[244] Today, the churches and the western democracies, too, agree with the Quakers. They realize use of force in matters of conscience is wrong, and the churches have acknowledged that they were wrong in the past to try to compel conversions, whether from heretics or non-Christians.

Barclay makes the telling and frightening point that, if the party in power believes it should destroy those who differ from it, "every possible means will be used to attain that power."[245] In other words, power will never pass peacefully from one party to another if the one that loses knows it faces torture and death. Barclay grasped that truth from the English civil war. Since then, democracies have learned to pass power peacefully, although political parties sometimes use methods not altogether honest, as captured by the modern proverb, "Vote early and often."

So, neither church nor state should use force against conscience, even if wrong, as long as persons and property are not in danger. Barclay reaches somewhat further than this, however, when he includes human society and its welfare. When these abstractions are threatened is more difficult to discern. However, Quakers have usually left political matters to the politicians and concentrated on how to live holy lives. Here, the testimonies take hold.

The testimonies

From the first, Quakers have tried to practice five testimonies. They are equality, truthfulness, simplicity, community, and peace. Four are treated here, with a separate section for the complex testimony of peace.

The most central testimony is equality. Everyone has the Light within. Therefore, everyone deserves equal respect. That is the Quaker position. Barclay explicitly says that equality does not entail communism, in which people share everything in common, or "leveling," the destruction of classes. He declares the relations between kings and people or parents and children should be maintained, that some are educated as servants and comfortable with coarse clothes and food, whereas others are better educated and accustomed to fine clothes and food. These differences are acceptable, as long as those with more refined tastes treat their possessions "without extravagance or waste."[246]

Equality of respect is a different matter. Fox believes God told him neither to doff his hat to the upper classes nor to address people with different pronouns according to class and intimacy, as custom then dictated, but to approach all equally, "all men and women, without any respect to rich or poor, great or small."[247] Moreover, he sincerely includes women as equals, as spelled out in his journal and elsewhere.[248] Nonetheless, even among the Quakers, the words of some carry more weight than those of others.

Barclay comments that behaviors then in fashion, such as kneeling, bowing, and removing one's hat before aristocrats and officials, are normally behaviors used in the worship of God and, therefore, unsuitably done before others. God created all people to be equal, so people should reserve such special honors for the deity.[249]

Equality of respect, but maintenance of classes, makes slavery an awkward issue for the early Quakers. The first Quakers accept the practice, as does the Bible. Slavery resembles servitude, and the first Quakers recognized the separate stations of master and servant. Yet, in a sermon preached in Barbados in 1671,[250] Fox addresses the issue with remarkable generosity and compassion. He starts by pointing out that Christ died for all people, whether black, tawny, white, Muslim, or barbarian. (Some slaves were Muslim, while others followed African religions, hence "barbarian.") He enjoins his hearers to consider their slaves members of their own families. They should preach to them and love them, for Christ enlightens them, too. He tells his listeners to free their slaves after a time, although they paid good money for them, and then not to send them away empty-handed. Finally, he suggests they treat their slaves as they would like to be treated, if they were slaves.

If enslaved, of course, his hearers would like to be free. This example is especially powerful for Fox's hearers, for some whites were slaves in Fox's time, and daring dangerous seas to reach Barbados, as Fox's hearers had, could end in capture and enslavement.

The testimony of truth telling seems simple enough: tell it, on all occasions, to high and low. However, telling the truth got the early Quakers into more trouble, perhaps, than any other activity.

Fox travels to towns on market days to preach because many people are there to hear him. Activities at market move him to preach to those buying and selling. Of one such occasion, he writes: "[I] there declared unto them that the day of the Lord was coming upon all their deceitful ways and doings and deceitful merchandise, and that they were to lay away all cozening and cheating and keep to 'yea' and 'nay', and speak the truth one to another."[251] The merchants surely resented being called cheats and liars.

Fox reports on the pastor of a church who complains bitterly to his congregation that Fox had enticed away "'all the honest men and women in Lancashire to him; and now', he said, 'he comes here to do the same.'" Fox replies, "'What have the priests left them, but such as themselves? For if it be the honest that receive the Truth and are turned to Christ, then it must be the dishonest that follow thee and such as thou art.'"[252] If the preacher told the truth about all the honest people flocking to Fox, then Fox is logically right, that the churches must have retained the dishonest. He speaks the truth without restraint to all, and meets threats and beatings for his trouble.

Yet, some things turn out well. Quaker truth telling in the marketplace began the single price system that suits the consumer so well in today's developed economies. As for Quaker merchants, although shunned at first because of their odd and impertinent ways, by 1653 customers sought them because they were so honest parents sent their children to buy from them, certain they would not be cheated. Soon, the Quakers' trade doubled compared with that of their neighbors.[253]

Telling the truth to all at all times meant not taking oaths. As Barclay observes, with impeccable logic, if people are truthful, oaths are unnecessary. If they are not, oaths are useless.[254]

Moreover, as Barclay notes, Jesus said not to swear (Matt. 5:33-37).[255] Some argued against him that passages in the Hebrew Scriptures (Deut. 6:13, 10:20; Lev. 19:12) either explicitly said God said to swear oaths, or not to swear false oaths, which allows swearing true ones. And if God so commanded, then Christ could not forbid it. Barclay answers,

> Some things are good because they are commanded, or evil because they are forbidden. Other things are commanded because they are good, or forbidden because they are evil. Circumcision and oaths were good when, and because, they were commanded, but for no other reason. When they were prohibited, and because they were prohibited under the gospel, they are evil.[256]

This is another example of the early Quakers' thinking in terms of dispensations, the times described in the Hebrew Scriptures being one dispensation, New Testament times another.

Their unwillingness to swear the required Oath of Allegiance to Charles II when monarchy returned to England in 1660 lumped the Quakers with other groups who refused to take the oath, some of whom plotted against Charles. A justice of the peace confronts Fox, asking him how to distinguish Quakers from the others who refuse to take the oath. Fox explains that the others will swear in some cases, but the Quakers never swear at all. If, for example, a thief steals the others' horses or cows, they will swear to the authorities that they are theirs, but Quakers cannot swear at all, not even to save their own goods.[257] Quakers were consistent, even to their own detriment.

Telling the truth meant not flattering others. Authorities flaunted flattering titles, such as Your Holiness, Your Majesty, Your Eminence, Your Excellency, Your Lordship, Your Honor. In many cases, the titles rang false. Your Honor might be dishonorable, Your Holiness profane, Your Excellency immoral. Therefore, Quakers eschew titles. Barclay observes that obedience due to superiors does not include addressing them by title. Nor does charity demand lies.[258] Thus, the early Quakers objected to lying, not to the class system.

Truth telling is a mark of simplicity. The early Quakers practice simplicity – what they called "plainness" – in other areas of daily life. Gwyn comments succinctly, "The Quaker life was often

as materially austere and plain as it was spiritually rich and color-ful."[259] However, the Quakers are not austere to be ascetics. For them, asceticism stems from human desires, not from God. Rather, plain dress is to free people from bondage to fashion, to display quietness and weightiness. To be weighty is to embrace the deep and lasting and to renounce whatever impedes these.[260]

Barclay comments that plain clothing does not imply people should dress alike. Their station in life, the climate of their country, and their physical needs matter. The point is not to dress the same, but to relinquish the unnecessary. He thinks people should wear what they can afford and dress in the natural products of their country. He rejects vanity and discontent. He remarks of people who wear ribbons and lace, makeup and fancy hairdos, "They apply themselves more to beautifying their bodies than to improving their souls." [261]

He also objects to most forms of recreation, like gambling, sports, and trifling plays. He claims they are a waste of time and end in fighting, profanity, and vulgarity. He suggests for recreation that people visit their friends, garden, perform scientific experiments, or read history.[262]

In summary, Barclay asks which activities promote being "humble, meek, and mortified," "very good, sober, mortified and self-denying." Are they fancy clothes, painted faces, jewelry, ribbons, and lace? Are they frivolous pleasures, dancing, gambling, singing, playing instruments, attending trivial plays, and lying?[263] Clearly, he thinks not. These things are worldly, and he rejects worldliness. He admires Quakers because "[God] has inwardly redeemed them from the world."[264]

Barclay is writing after the Restoration of 1660 when Puritans no longer govern Britain, and many entertainments earlier suppressed are in full flower. Yet Fox, writing before 1660, during the Commonwealth, takes a similar perspective. As a young man of twenty-five, he spends his time

In warning such as kept public houses for entertainment that they should not let people have more drink than would do them good, and in testifying against their wakes or feasts, their May-games, sports, plays, and shows, which trained up people to vanity and looseness, and led them from the fear of God, and the days they had set forth for holy-days were usually the times wherein they most dishonoured God by these things.[265]

This is 1649, the year the Puritans beheaded Charles I!

Six years later, at the height of the Commonwealth, Fox addresses a letter "To such as follow after the fashions of the world." Men wear jewelry, lace, and ribbons, and powder their hair. Women sport jewelry, too, and paint "spots on their faces, noses, cheeks, foreheads." They dress up, he judges, like actors. Such inanity receives respect from the worldly – bared heads and deferential bows. The problems are not only vanity and pride. These frivolous fools squander resources. They are the "spoilers of the creation, and have the fat and the best of it, and waste and destroy it." He complains that owners place ribbons on their horses' heads and rings in their ears, but especially that they race their mounts to the point of ruin.[266] It does seem a vain, foolish, and profligate world.

Quaker simplicity reaches to matters more vital than dress and entertainment. It touches business. Fox assembles people of similar trades to consider how to be more godly in their vocations. Quakers institute the single price system. Some change their occupations because the occupations themselves encourage frivolity, like making or selling lace or jewelry. John Woolman, tailor and retail tradesman, sells only necessities. Later, finding his trade expanding too much, he sells it and retains only his tailor's shop because tailoring is a simple occupation that allows more time for spiritual pursuits.[267]

This is the same John Woolman who convinces Quakers of the sinfulness of owning slaves, so Quakers free their slaves, and some become anti-slavery crusaders. His sense of slavery's wrongfulness begins when he is twenty-three and his employer asks him to write out a bill of sale of a slave. He does, but his conscience aches afterwards. Later, he journeys into the southern part of North America and sees people living in ease and luxury on the labor of slaves. He finds this wrong. He raises several objections. Slaves manage marriages among themselves, while the owners ignore the slaves' arrangements and sunder couples in distant sales. The labor is heavy, and overseers whip the slaves, often disciplining them severely, to the point of impairment. Meanwhile, the slaves have little to wear and less to eat, much of it raised themselves on Sundays, their supposed day of rest. Not only do their owners fail to teach them to read, they discourage literacy. Those, Woolman says, who know the God of Jesus Christ who is merciful and benevolent "will therein perceive that the indignation of God is kindled against oppression and cruelty, and in beholding the great distress of so numerous a people will find cause for mourning.[268] He finds cause for reform. One of the reforms he would institute is simpler living, so less slave labor is needed.[269]

Woolman's compassion and concern for others is a mark of community, the fourth Quaker testimony. The fourth testimony recapitulates the others. In a community committed to the testimonies, people treat others as equals, which eliminates pridefulness, boasting, and derision. They tell the truth, which eradicates cheating, lying, and deception. All live simply, without frivolity and without waste. Thus, they live within their means. In keeping with contemporary interests, today's Quakers try to live ecologically, but the concern with wasting and destroying the Earth extends back to Fox. He finds wasting the creation sinful. As we know now, it is also dangerous for Earth's species, including our own. Finally, in keeping with the peace testimony, the Quaker community is peaceful.

The peace testimony

According to Cooper, the Quaker peace testimony has three components. Individuals experience peace inwardly, with themselves and the Light within. Next, individuals live at peace outwardly, among themselves. Finally, peace pervades the public order, and safety reigns.[270]

Barclay declares love maintains peace. Not only should we love God as if we are in love, we should love others, even our enemies, as Jesus taught. We should not destroy them, as if we are animals, but use reason and show patience, charity, and forbearance. War and war-like behavior is worldly, for it involves violence, deceit, and injustice, which are ungodly activities.[271]

Fox makes his first statements on war in 1651 when he is in prison. Cromwell's supporters invite, even beg, him to become a captain in the army of the Commonwealth because of his bravery. Thus, he will avoid more prison. However, he remarks,

> I told them I lived in the virtue of that life and power that took away the occasion of all wars, and I know from whence all wars

did rise, from the lust according to James's doctrine [James 4:1].
. . . I was come into the covenant of peace which was before
wars and strifes were.[272]

Fox explains that he lives in the Light and, so, is free of sinful
desires that cause war. Inwardly, he lives in paradise as Adam and
Eve did before the Fall (in "the covenant of peace which was before
wars and strifes were").

Later, after the defeat of the king's army, Cromwell asks Fox to
declare that he will not fight against him. Fox promises in writing.
He does so in words that probably surprised Cromwell. He calls
himself "The son of God who is sent to stand a witness against all
violence."[273]

When the king returns, his minions accuse Fox of plotting
against him. Fox replies that he is no enemy to anyone, including
the king. "But I am in the love that fulfills the law and thinks no
evil, but loves enemies and would have the King saved and come
to the knowledge of the Truth."[274] Upon entering court sometime
after, he announces, "'Peace be among you'", then declares, "I
never learned the postures of war, and I loved all men; I was enemy
to no man."[275]

The early Quakers loved each other sufficiently that, when many
are in prison (and the prisons are vile), some two hundred free
Quakers go to Parliament and offer to take the places of their imprisoned friends. Parliament refuses, and even whips some to make
them go away.[276] What a strange scene it must have been!

Those in power sometimes mistook Quakers for a revolutionary sect known as the Fifth Monarchy Men, the four former monar-
chies being Assyria, Persia, Greece, and Rome (Dan. 2:36-45).
They believed Christ was to come immediately and establish the
fifth monarchy that would last a thousand years (Rev. 20:4). They
rose against Cromwell in 1657 and against King Charles II in 1661,
who beheaded the leaders, so the sect disappeared. After the 1661
uprising, the leading Quakers penned a letter to the King, dated
21st day, 11th month 1660 (January 1661 in the present calendar),
known as the *Declaration of 1660*. A dozen Quakers signed it, Fox
among them. The *Declaration* constitutes the first published statement against war by the community of Quakers. Here are some
excerpts to capture its essence.

Our principle is, and our practices have always been, to seek peace and ensue it and to follow after righteousness and the knowledge of God, seeking the good and welfare and doing that which tends to the peace of all. We know that wars and fightings proceed from the lusts of men (as Jas. iv. 1-3), out of which lusts the Lord hath redeemed us, and so out of the occasion of war. . . . All bloody principles and practices, we, as to our own particulars, do utterly deny, with all outward wars and strife and fightings with outward weapons, for any end or under any pretence whatsoever. . . .

The spirit of Christ, which leads us into all Truth, will never move us to fight and war against any man with outward weapons, neither for the kingdom of Christ, nor for the kingdoms of this world. . . .

And as for the kingdoms of this world, we cannot covet them, much less can we fight for them. . . .

For this we can say to the whole world, we have wronged no man's person or possessions, we have used no force nor violence against any man, we have been found in no plots, nor guilty of sedition. When we have been wronged, we have not sought to revenge ourselves, we have not made resistance against authority, but wherein we could not obey for conscience' sake, we have suffered even the most of any people in the nation. We have been accounted as sheep for the slaughter, persecuted and despised, beaten, stoned, wounded, stocked, whipped, imprisoned, haled out of synagogues, cast into dungeons and noisome vaults where many have died in bonds, shut up from our friends, denied needful sustenance for many days together, with other the like cruelties.

And the cause of all this our sufferings is not for any evil, but for things relating to the worship of our God and in obedience to his requirings of us. For which cause we shall freely give up our bodies a sacrifice, rather than disobey the Lord. . . .

Our meetings were stopped and broken up in the days of Oliver [Cromwell], in pretence of plotting against him; . . . and now we are called plotters against King Charles. . . . We have suffered all along because we would not take up carnal [physical] weapons to fight withal against any, and are thus made a prey upon because we are the innocent lambs of Christ and cannot avenge ourselves.[277]

Echoing Fox – and Barclay before Barclay puts pen to paper – they say God has rescued them from worldly desires. Why, then, would they fight for a worldly kingdom? Instead, they stand for God's reign of peace toward all, here and now, even to death.

Their reasons for opposing war are biblical, but they are also characterological. Barclay comments that to be a warrior is to engage in deceit, violence, injustice, and revenge.[278] Quakers eschew these characteristics. Three centuries later, Brinton observes that Quakers are pacifists, not because loss of life and property are evil (they can be good!), but because of the spiritual evils war fosters, such as deceit, hatred, and brutality.[279] The Quakers are not alone in this belief. Many famous figures intimately concerned with war write of the evils of character that arise from being a soldier, among them Thucydides, Clausewitz, Lincoln, and Tolstoy.[280]

When others object that self-defense is natural, and religion does not annihilate nature, Barclay replies that not to defend oneself is, indeed, contrary to nature. It is the perfection of Christian faith, for "it demands self-denial, and placing one's entire confidence in God."[281]

Brinton notes that the Quakers' stand against violence is not only against war. Quakers promote nonviolence in prisons, mental hospitals, and schools; in the state through encouragement of democracy; and internationally.[282] They work against violence between the races and against women.[283] Quaker Meetings are nonviolent not only because there is no physical aggression, but because no one is sarcastic or shouts others down. The peace testimony rejects violence of all kinds. Therefore, many Quakers are vegetarians.

Numerous comments and quotations from the early Quakers in these chapters on the origins and stable core of Quakerism demonstrate that they believed scripture is inspired and true, and they tried to follow it, especially the New Testament. Since the seventeenth century, however, biblical scholarship has questioned the Bible's inspiration and its truth. Now that the theology of early Quakerism lies exposed, we can ask how well it withstands modern biblical criticism.

SUMMARY OF THE STABLE CORE

The foundational Quaker doctrine is that all people have a measure of divine Light within them. This doctrine springs from the Quaker experience of personal transformation combined with humility and attention to others. Humility says, if I possess the Light, then so must everyone. Attention to others shows that pagan philosophers like Plato and Aristotle had it. So do good people of other faiths or no faith. Moreover, the Light transforms evil people into good ones, so evil people must have it, too, at least as a seed.

The remainder of the core Quaker theology follows logically from this foundational doctrine. Because the Light is divine, everyone should heed it. To heed it, people must listen for it, and a good listener listens in silence, without distractions. Hence, silent Quaker Meetings for Worship developed, without the distractions of liturgy or outward sacraments. In Meeting, Quakers commune inwardly with the Light.

Furthermore, if everyone has a measure of the Light, then logically, everyone deserves equal respect. To live as if everyone deserves equal respect results in the Quaker testimonies of equality, truth telling (to deceive is disrespectful and manipulative), simplicity (lack of self-display, for self-display announces one's superiority), and peace (for violence violates the other person and ruins one's own character). Practiced together, these testimonies produce peaceful Quaker communities of mutual cooperators, with all their individuality and diversity. As they try to live together in respect and peace, Quakers look for the Light to inform their communal decisions, just as it informs their individual ones. This communal effort results in Quaker Meetings for Worship for Business and other collective enterprises.

PART II

SCRIPTURE: THE CHALLENGE OF RATIONAL CRITICISM

PEOPLE LIVING in seventeenth century Christendom believe the Bible narrates history. To all, Adam and Eve are real people, the first couple, who disobey God and bring evil into God's good creation. Noah survives a worldwide flood with his family in an ark built at God's command and saves all the species that otherwise would have gone extinct. Moses receives commandments from God on Mount Sinai. David consolidates a kingdom, and his son Solomon builds the first Jewish Temple in Jerusalem. The Babylonians defeat the Jews and carry their leaders into exile in Babylon. The Jews return by decree of Cyrus and rebuild the Temple. Jesus is born in Bethlehem, baptized by John the Baptist, and is crucified under Pilate for human sins. God raises him from the dead, and he ascends to the heavens. Seventeenth century Christians accept each of these events as equally historical.

Nonetheless, Protestant and Catholic parted a century earlier at the Reformation over various theological and ecclesiastical matters. Quakers found the Reformation insufficient. They thought Protestants, even the Calvinist Presbyterians and the Baptists who rejected infant baptism, remained too Catholic. Quakers considered Quakerism the third way, neither Protestant nor Catholic, although containing elements of both.

The remainder of this book honors the Quaker distinction and generally treats Catholic and Protestant together under the head of "Christian orthodoxy" (or merely "orthodoxy"). This means orthodoxy theology, which is complex and nuanced, is necessarily simplified. Where I feel the simplification leans toward distortion, I correct in endnotes. The simplification aids in drawing the relevant distinctions between orthodoxy and Quakerism. Some who call themselves Quakers today will object to this distinction, crying that they are orthodox Christians. And so they are.

The nineteenth century saw Quakerism split into factions. It remains fractured today. The fundamental division is between Christ-centered Quakerism, which theologically (and often liturgically) is orthodox Protestantism, and Quaker universalism. Theologically, Quaker universalism represents the original Quakerism of Fox and Barclay, which, as we have seen, is unorthodox – rightly so, it thinks, for it finds orthodoxy defective when compared to the Christianity of the New Testament. In Christ-centered Quakerism, salvation occurs after death and then only for believers in Christ's salvic action as a sacrifice for sin. In Christian orthodoxy, Christ saves believers only. In Quaker universalism, as in Barclay and Fox, all people have the divine Light within, and all can experience salvation here and now, whatever their religion, sex, color, or sexual orientation, if only they heed the Light. To Quaker universalists, as to Fox and Barclay, people's theological beliefs are, on the whole, unimportant.

The early Quakers united the divergent Christian beliefs of later factions by equating the Light with Jesus Christ, as foretold by the prophets and presented in the New Testament. Their God and Christ resided not in heaven but in human hearts, or, perhaps more accurately, not only in heaven, but also in human hearts, as foretold by the prophets and presented in the New Testament.

Modern biblical criticism is skeptical of the Bible as history, prophecy, or authority. Modern biblical critics are academics. They examine the Bible employing the same critical, academic tools wielded on secular works, seeking who wrote it, when, where, and why. They approach the Bible with textual methods applicable to secular literary and historical works combined, where appropriate, with extra-biblical history plus archaeological, anthropological, sociological, cosmological, geological, and biological information. The result has destroyed much of the creditability of the Bible.

To simplify, the narrative stretching from Genesis 1:1 to or through the reign of David is not historical, although the narratives of Jewish slavery in Egypt, the Exodus, settlement in the hills of Palestine, and the united kingdom under David and Solomon may point to some genuine events. The Torah and the Deuteronomistic History (Genesis through 2 Kings) were probably composed under Josiah in the seventh century B.C.E. Although using older documents and oral histories, the author/editor(s) handled them freely, ignoring some, combining two or more versions, adding transitions and comments, all with an agenda – to further Josiah's political and religious goals. Various author/editors with different agendas revised these documents again during the Exile of the sixth century B.C.E. and later. The Jews began to consider other documents sacred, especially the prophetic works in our current Bible, literature dealing with the end times, and other works simply referred to as "the writings." However, even in the first century B.C.E., neither the text nor the canon of the Hebrew Scriptures was established. The Jewish canon stabilized only in the second or third centuries C.E., the Christian in the third or fourth centuries. Although Christianity sprang from Jesus and beliefs about him, the New Testament is largely theological rather than historical. Nonetheless, biblical scholarship, combined with the tools mentioned above, can offer a substantiated sketch of the man Jesus.[284]

The second part of this book, then, asks which viewpoint fits best with modern biblical scholarship, the orthodox Christian or the Quaker. This part of the book consists of four chapters that compare Quakerism and orthodoxy on the Fall, salvation, the authority of scripture, and the universality of grace. It begins at the beginning, with the Fall of Adam and Eve. Because I have treated the Fall and original sin in detail elsewhere,[285] here I only sketch those elements relevant to the question at issue.

6: THE FALL OF ADAM AND EVE

THE SEVENTEENTH century considered the narrative of Adam and Eve, as well as the theology built upon it, history. The narrative occurs in Genesis 2 and 3. In brief, God tells Adam not to eat the fruit of the tree of the knowledge of good and evil, saying he will die that day if he does. Then God creates Eve. They disobey, Eve eating first and handing the fruit to Adam. God curses them, Adam with labor in farming, Eve with labor in childbirth. God then expels them from Eden, where they were created, and places angels and a flaming sword at the gate to keep them from returning to eat the fruit of the tree of life and attain immortality. Orthodox Christianity offers one interpretation of the narrative.[286]

Orthodox Christianity

For orthodox Christianity, Adam and Eve's disobedience constitutes a Fall that results in the corruption of human nature. Orthodoxy holds not only that Eve and Adam's corrupt and sinful nature passes to their progeny, their guilt does too. Catholics solve the problem of infant guilt through the sacrament of baptism, where the guilt is washed away,[287] while Protestants solve it through the concept of imputed (attributed) grace. Protestants claim human beings cannot change, for we are totally corrupt. All are eternally worthy of damnation. However, in looking at those God decides to save, God sees Jesus' obedience and attributes that graceful act to them.[288] In contrast, when viewing the damned, God sees only their corruption. Orthodoxy believes Jesus saves people from God's wrath at Adam and Eve's disobedience and our consequent sinfulness through his atoning sacrifice on the cross that, somehow, appeases God's anger. Protestantism and Catholicism differ as to how.

65

Influenced by modern biblical criticism, liberal orthodox Christians interpret the narrative of Adam and Eve as metaphor rather than history. They say the narrative reveals the human condition, one of estrangement from God and alienation from nature and each other. They view our lives on Earth as a time of sojourning and testing. Earth is not our home. Our home is heaven, which we enter after death. Treating the Fall as metaphor, of course, destroys the doctrine of the atonement. Jesus' literal, historical crucifixion might atone for a literal, historical sin, but hardly for a metaphorical one by a fictitious pair. If the narrative is metaphor, why is God angry with us? How did we become estranged? When did evil enter the world? Are we responsible? With the narrative no longer historical, a host of such questions arises.

The early Quakers largely disagree with orthodoxy. Barclay articulates the Quaker position.

Quakerism

Writing before the rise of science and biblical criticism, Barclay agrees with conservative orthodoxy that the Fall is history. Adam and Eve are real people who disobey God, and God casts them out of Eden. Their nature is corrupted and, through them, all human nature. However, Barclay interprets God's threat of death upon eating the fruit of good and evil spiritually. When God says, "of the tree of the knowledge of good and evil you shall not eat, for in the day that you eat of it you shall die" (Gen. 2:17), God is not referring to physical death because Adam lives afterwards for hundreds of years and God does not lie. Rather, says Barclay, "the penalty for that act must have been a spiritual one."[289]

Then, with amazing nonchalance, he dismisses the literal reading of the narrative:

> Now whatever literal significance that may have, we may safely ascribe a mystical significance to the paradise it describes and consider it to be really the spiritual communion and fellowship which those who have faith obtain with God through Jesus Christ. To them only do the cherubim [guarding the gate of Eden] give way, and to as many as enter by him who calls himself the Door (John 10:7-9).[290]

Barclay treats the narrative as metaphor. Spiritual communion with God is lost at the Fall. Moreover, it is reclaimable. Those who want to return to this paradisiacal state of divine communion must merely go through the door, Jesus Christ. They can enter now. For Barclay, salvation is readily (although not easily) available. He echoes Fox in Fox's claim to resemble Adam before the Fall, or Jesus, tempted but persevering.

Yet, Barclay acknowledges the narrative's historical consequences. He believes human nature is corrupt and people in their natural state cannot understand spiritual matters.[291] However, he rejects the generation-to-generation transmission of Eve and Adam's guilt. Babies who die unbaptized are neither damned nor enter the Catholic limbo. Rather, only sinful actions generate guilt.[292] The Quakers hold individuals responsible for their behavior, their sins, and their guilt before God.

Why? They agree with orthodoxy that human nature alone can do no good,[293] but they think human nature is not alone. Everyone has the Light within, the divine seed, to teach and lead people into the spiritual life, if only they listen for the divine voice.

Because the Quakers spiritualize the death God promises Adam, they probably think physical death natural. The narrative in Genesis 2 and 3 is notoriously ambiguous on the subject, yet its main thrust seems to be that we are naturally mortal. God promises Adam death "in the day that you eat," but Adam lives on. God curses Adam with agricultural labor until he dies (Gen. 3:17-20), not with death itself. And later, God worries that Eve and Adam might eat the fruit of the tree of life and gain immortality (Gen. 3:22), so he casts them out of Eden where the tree grows, implying that they were created mortal, that mortality is their natural state. So, if the Quakers consider death natural, their thoughts are flowing with strong currents of the text – and with the theology of Eastern Christianity.[294]

Moreover, even if Adam and Eve suffer spiritual death when they eat the fruit, forfeiting communion with God for themselves and their progeny, the Quakers think spiritual resurrection possible. Sit in the Light, turn from wrongdoing, enter the door of Eden, smell paradise before the Fall. The divine seed within can grow, will grow, if only people turn to it and follow its leading. The Quakers treat their spiritual, metaphorical meaning of the narrative of Adam and Eve as primary. Quaker experience tells them everyone can conquer spiritual alienation and enjoy communion with God now, in this life. The natural human condition may be one of alienation from conscious communion with God, but all are already in relationship with the divine seed and, if they choose, may consciously experience communion here and now. The natural human condition can attain spirituality if only people attend to the Light within.

The early Quakers thus integrate what today would be the conservative and liberal orthodox views, but with a difference. They think human nature is transmitted through the generations, as the orthodox do. (Today, we might think of the stable characteristics of a species.) However, they reject the idea that guilt infects progeny across generations. (Today, we might think of the impossibility of the inheritance of acquired characteristics.) Moreover, they believe salvation available now, universally. Immersed in Christian theology as he is, Barclay thinks believing it unnecessary to salvation. Such views enable Quakerism to withstand the assaults of modern biblical criticism.

Modern biblical criticism

Modern biblical criticism takes two approaches to the narrative of Genesis 2 and 3. Most importantly, biblical criticism finds the narrative unhistorical, metaphor rather than event. Science shows the universe to be very old, some 13.7 billion years, Earth about 4.6 billion years old, and evolution a protracted process beginning with unicellular organisms. Multicellular organisms evolved slowly. Among them, we are late arrivals.

The modern Catholic Church insists, nonetheless, a first couple existed who sinned, from whom we are descended and whose guilt and corrupted nature we inherit. However, evolution does not occur in individuals, but among groups. It is a statistical affair. Science suggests that the "first humans" emerged from a population of at least ten thousand individuals. Indeed, science makes speaking of "first humans" anachronistic because evolution is a gradual process, usually, and certainly so in mammals.

Without Adam and Eve as actual people who literally sinned, orthodox theology falls apart. We did not cause our own downfall, and Jesus is not the second Adam as St. Paul asserts in 1 Corinthians 15:45-59, for there was no first Adam. Jesus' obedience cannot atone for Adam's disobedience, as orthodox theology interprets Philippians 2:8.

The other approach is to read the text carefully to see whether it supplies firm foundations for the theology allegedly erected on it. It does not. Orthodox theology says human nature degenerated. The text says human nature improved!

Here are the proofs. First, the primordial couple eats the fruit of the tree of knowledge, thus acquiring knowledge. Many theologians simply ignore this, or even claim – flatly against the text – that they lose knowledge, but others notice and try to make the knowledge itself an evil acquisition. The text will not allow this, however, for God disagrees: "Then the Lord God said, 'See, the man has become like one of us, knowing good and evil'" (Gen. 3:22). Assuming God is good, if Eve and Adam became more like God, they become better through the knowledge of good and evil.

Second, God assumes they might eat of the tree of life and become immortal, turning themselves into gods, so clearly they are climbing the chain of being, not descending. God exiles them from Eden where the tree of life grows precisely to keep them from ascending further.

Third, the tendency of theology in the West during Christianity's first centuries was increasingly to claim God created Eve and Adam flawless, until Augustine (354-430) declared them created perfect. However, their perfection is not in the text. They are, after all, dust: "then the Lord God formed man from the dust of the ground" (Gen. 2:7); "you [shall] return to the ground, for out of it you were taken; you are dust, and to dust you shall return,'" God intones (Gen. 3:19). They are also naive, for they are newly created, lacking experience, and therefore easily seduced.[295] To be so vulnerable is hardly perfection. They have room to improve, and knowledge would raise them out of their ignorance.

But, what about Genesis 1? There God calls creation good. There, God creates human beings in the divine image (1:26). Surely, these passages suggest perfection.

They do. However, Genesis 1 is a separate narrative from the narrative of the Fall in Genesis 2 and 3, written at a different time by different people. In the original Hebrew of each, God even has a different name, signaled in English by the use of "God" in Genesis

1 and "Lord God" in Genesis 2 and 3. Modern scholarship disallows reading Genesis 1 as a prelude to Genesis 2 and 3.

In conservative orthodox theology, Genesis 2 and 3 combined with Genesis 1 do a lot of work. First, the narratives explain the origins of things – God created them. Second, they depict a good God who created a good world. Third, they describe how evil came into the world, blaming the creatures rather than the creator. Fourth, they offer a theory of human nature. Finally, they proffer a reason life sometimes does seem cursed, and evil sometimes seems like punishment.

However, the theology distorts the text. In the narrative, evil begins not with Eve and Adam but with the serpent, the tempter whom God curses first, but the narrative offers no explanation for the serpent's evil. Moreover, if perfect, the first couple would not succumb so easily. Furthermore, Adam and Eve's nature is not corrupted, but improves.

Worse for orthodox theology, the events never occurred. They are not history, but literature, usually classified as myth, a kind of metaphor.

Liberal orthodox theology acknowledges the metaphorical character of the narratives and treats them as separate stories. For it, Genesis 2 and 3 tell us about the human condition, that we are alienated from God and far from home. Certainly, the narrative is a metaphor of alienation. God exiles Eve and Adam from the only home they have known and, presumably, does not walk in the land east of Eden in the cool of the day, as was God's habit in Eden (Gen. 3:8).

God's curse of Adam, however, fails to describe the human condition. It describes only one way of life, a life of hard agricultural labor. It neglects to describe the lives of hunter-gatherers that preceded agricultural ways of life by several hundred thousand years, lives in industrial factories, lives of commerce, or lives spent before computer screens, manipulating information. God's curse of Eve is more broadly applicable, for women have labored in childbirth from the time our brains grew large. Yet, effective birth control, modern anesthetics, and caesarian sections ease the pain, and women are slowly liberating themselves from the curse of patriarchy (Gen. 3:16).

However, liberal theologians generally ignore the actual curses in Genesis 3, thereby distorting the text again. And, of course, we are at home. We evolved here on Earth. The blood in our veins derives from the salt water of primordial seas. The big bang and the stars created the elements in our bodies. We are intimate parts of this universe, not aliens.

Therefore, Christian orthodoxy fails under modern biblical criticism. The only truth it offers is our lack of communion with God, and special revelation is hardly required to tell us that.

In contrast, seventeenth century Quakerism succeeds remarkably well. Like conservative orthodoxy, it sees the Genesis narratives as history, but the Bible is only a secondary source of revelation in Quakerism. Moreover, Quakerism's primary use of the narrative is metaphorical, in full agreement with modern biblical criticism. The main problem lies in the interpretation of the metaphor.

Liberal orthodoxy's interpretation touches only one part of the text, the exile from Eden. It offers no treatment within the narrative for our alienation or our sinful state, which it largely ignores. The cure it offers occurs outside the narrative and only in salvation after death. In contrast, early Quakerism interprets the metaphor as both diagnosis and remedy. It says, yes, we are sinful and alienated from God, but not so sinful and alienated that reconciliation is impossible. The germ of our reconciliation lies within everyone, for all possess the divine seed. Our condition is temporary. We can return to Eden, here and now. If we focus inward, heed the divine voice within, repent our sins, and wait in the divine Light, it will enlighten and heal us. Communion with God is available now.

At its most hopeful, liberal orthodoxy has us sojourning toward the divine until we encounter it after death or at the end of the world in the general resurrection. Quakerism invites us to rejoice in the divine Light today. One of early Quakerism's favorite biblical passages is Jeremiah 31:33-34.

> But this is the covenant that I will make with the house of Israel after those days, says the Lord. I will put my law within them, and I will write it on their hearts; and I will be their God, and they shall be my people. No longer shall they teach one another, or say to each other, "Know the Lord," for they shall all know me, from the least of them to the greatest, says the Lord.

No longer will the external, written law be necessary. It will become internal, and each can learn it directly from God. This is Quakerism's belief.

Because Quakerism stands on individual and collective experience of the presence of God, it is largely independent of traditional Christian theology. Speculation, says Fox, consists of "notions" gleaned from others and from books, including the Bible, and he challenges us to speak for ourselves, out of our own experience. Scripture is unnecessary, Fox proclaims. Those who never read it, who have not heard of Jesus, can find salvation, here and now, by turning to the Light within. The great American Quaker, John Woolman, visits the natives of the land to discover what they can teach him about the Spirit, although they remain unacquainted with the Bible.[296]

Today, our story of origins is the saga that stretches from the big bang to our evolution (see chapter 11). The human condition is not that of cursed Adam laboring in the fields. Rather, it is quite variable, depending as it does on economics and technology. Science is answering questions about human nature through neurological research and experimental and evolutionary psychology. Evolution and evolutionary psychology tell us far more about the source and cause of evil than Genesis 3 does (see chapter 12).

Yet, despite these changes in our outlook since the seventeenth century, the core of Quaker theology stands firm. The facts that the big bang and the stars created the elements of our bodies and we evolved naturally from other species do not preclude our having a divine seed within that is not a product of evolution. Perhaps the divine suffuses all nature, but we are the only creatures who become conscious of it, who are able to follow its leading deliberately.

Biblical criticism never shakes the core of Quakerism, for the core of Quaker theology is experiential. The belief that the Light within transforms people is true to Quaker experience. Quakers do not need the Bible to substantiate their testimonies, for they follow logically from the central belief, based on experience, of the Light within. Although Quakerism grew up with the Bible as history, the disproof of the historicity of Adam and Eve and their Fall fails to disturb. All Quakerism requires is for our nature to be inclined to worldliness, needing divine aid to live a spiritual life. Quakerism also survives biblical criticism focused on the orthodox doctrine(s) of salvation.

7. SALVATION

THE CHRISTIAN doctrine of salvation describes how Jesus Christ rescues humanity. It includes the doctrine(s) of the atonement that tells how he saves us from God's wrath and the doctrine(s) of grace that explains how he frees us from our own sin. The two are connected: God is angry because we are sinful. These doctrines, in turn, depend on a theory of human nature, in orthodox Christianity a nature corrupted by the Fall, the subject of the preceding chapter. While orthodoxy largely centers on the two poles of the Fall and the atonement, Quakerism emphasizes grace that returns us to the state of Adam and Eve before the Fall, if we do not resist it. Orthodoxy professes our sinful state and our alienation from God, remedied by the saving death of Jesus Christ on the cross, but realized only after death or at the general resurrection. Quakerism proclaims salvation through the growth of the divine seed within us that produces personal transformation, social cooperation, and unity with God, here and now. Meanwhile, modern biblical criticism concentrates on the authorship, sources, dates, and accuracy of texts. Yet, modern New Testament scholarship affects the doctrine(s) of salvation, especially that of orthodoxy.

Orthodoxy

As the last chapter comments, orthodoxy views human nature as corrupt, alienated from God, and in need of salvation. However, under the doctrine(s) of the atonement, salvation is a transaction between God and Christ, while people wait on the sidelines. Under orthodoxy, Protestant or Catholic, Jesus Christ's sacrifice on the cross removes God's anger at humanity, renders forgiveness and salvation possible, and enables God to treat at least some people as righteous. The technical term for this is *justification*. Although we remain unrighteous, we are justified in God's sight.

In contrast, grace is the assistance God offers us for our sanctification, wherein we actually become righteous. In Quaker terms, the Light within is God's grace in us.

In Protestantism, God imputes grace, but does not bestow it. God views the saved through the merits of Jesus Christ on the cross, but they remain unrighteous and unable to do good works. They are justified but not sanctified.[297] Nonetheless, God's grace is irresistible, a logical deduction, for how could a person resist grace that remains unbestowed?

For Catholics, grace flows from God through the church by means of the sacraments. The central, repeated sacrament is the Eucharist (Mass), which reenacts the sacrifice of Jesus Christ on the cross and offers repentant recipients the actual body and blood of Christ that works within them toward their sanctification. People can cooperate with God and perform good works. They can also resist God's grace, at least some forms of it.

In neither Catholicism nor Protestantism are grace and salvation available to everyone. For Protestants, individuals must have faith in Jesus' saving act to be saved, while for Catholics salvation comes only through the church.[298] Clearly, in either case, the persons saved need to know about Jesus (history) and accept his sacrifice (theology). On the doctrine of salvation, early Quakerism disagrees with much in both theologies.

Quakerism

The early Quakers view human nature as corrupt, inclined toward evil, and in need of salvation. They so strongly emphasize salvation through grace – the Light within – that the orthodox accuse them of neglecting Jesus Christ's saving atonement on the cross. Moreover, they believe the Light, unresisted, with the individual's cooperation, can save everyone.[299]

The orthodox emphasize the universality of sin. Our first parents sinned. Everyone is their progeny. All inherit their nature and their guilt. This is true whether people know of Adam, Eve, and the Fall or not.

The Quakers declare salvation is equally universal.[300] As those ignorant of Adam and Eve are, nonetheless, caught in their chains of sin, so those ignorant of Jesus Christ may be captured in his net of salvation.[301] Barclay adds, quite sensibly, that the gospel proclaims good news, bringing glad tidings and great joy to all people (Luke 2:10).[302] Yet, Protestantism damns the majority of humanity. If most are damned, the gospel would constitute bad news for most people.[303] Moreover, although helpful, knowledge of neither history nor theology is necessary for salvation. Such knowledge is outward, whereas only inward knowledge saves.[304]

Given this universalist theology and the many evil people who inhabit the globe, it becomes obvious that the Quakers consider people capable of defying grace, opposing the Light within. Barclay says the Light "can be resisted and rejected."[305] However, if people do not resist it, it produces in them a desire to cooperate with it,[306] and such cooperation results in the beginning of purity and the fruits of good works, which spring from the Spirit, not from human will.[307]

Barclay also states that Jesus Christ's death removes God's wrath over sins, which are both forgiven and eradicated.[308] Thus, Barclay retains atonement theology in the story of salvation.

In Barclay, then, salvation becomes a dual process.[309] On one side stands the saving act of Jesus Christ, removing God's anger. On the other shines the Light within, divine grace transforming people, purifying them, enabling them to do good works. Protestants deny God's transforming grace, so Fox tells a story to vivify Quaker reasoning:

> People are saved by Christ, they [Protestants] say, but while you are upon earth you must not be made free from sin. This is as much as if one should be in Turkey a slave, chained to a boat [as a galley slave], and one should come to redeem him to go into his own country; but say the Turks, 'Thou art redeemed, but whilst thou art upon the earth thou must not go out of Turkey, nor have the chain off thee.'. . .
>
> But I say you are redeemed by Christ. It cost him his blood to purchase man out of this state he is in, in the Fall, and bring him up to the state man was in before he fell . . . and not only thither, but to a state in Christ that shall never fall.[310]

Therefore, for Fox and Barclay, salvation is incomplete or even a lying tale unless it is effective and effected here, in this life.

Fox's small story demonstrates once more that early Quakerism was not a religion of doctrines or statements about the historical Jesus. Rather, people are to experience Spirit and receive its liberating power. Quakerism is a way of dealing with evil, transmuting it by love and creative energy and, sometimes, by suffering.[311] In early Quakerism, people are to possess Jesus, to incarnate him now[312] rather than merely to believe things about him.

As Douglas Gwyn notes, this theology is an atonement theology in several respects. Fox emphasizes the cross and, therefore, the death of iniquity, but also the death of the corrupt self. Moreover, the early Quakers themselves experience an atoning suffering. Finally, their lives of friendship, equality, and simplicity place them in conflict with the surrounding culture. They believe they are fighting the Lamb's war (Rev. 17:14) against worldliness.[313] Yet, as Gwyn's comments make clear, the early Quakers place most emphasis on personal and social transformation and deemphasize the cross. Instead, they center their theology on personal experience, and no one experiences Jesus' death but Jesus. Rather, the early Quakers rely on the Light within, the death of their own tendencies to wrongdoing, and personal transformation. They find these prefigured metaphorically in Jesus' death and resurrection.

Although modern New Testament scholarship deals primarily with textual questions rather than theological ones, Quakerism is more compatible with it than orthodoxy is.

Modern New Testament scholarship

Modern New Testament scholarship assumes the New Testament is a collection of documents human beings wrote and compiled. Indeed, every Christian can identify one of the authors, St. Paul. That human beings wrote the documents does not imply they are uninspired, but it does imply that scholars can approach them with the tools they apply to secular works. In doing so, the scholars solved four difficult problems the New Testament poses.

First, they separated the authentic Pauline letters from those attributed to Paul but written by others. The authentic letters are (in probable order of composition) 1 Thessalonians, Philippians, Philemon, Galatians, 1 Corinthians, 2 Corinthians, and Romans. Possibly 2 Thessalonians and Colossians are also authentic. The pseudonymous letters are Ephesians, 1 and 2 Timothy, and Titus.

Second, they dated the Gospels and the letters. Here, the Gospels are of most interest. All the authors of the Gospels seem to know about the chaos of Jewish civil/Roman war and (with the possible exception of Mark) the resulting destruction of Jerusalem in 70 C.E. Mark, then, is first, around 68-70; Matthew and Luke/Acts next, around 80-90, and John last, in the 90's.

Third, they solved the synoptic problem. Matthew, Mark, and Luke constitute the synoptic Gospels, which repeat much of the same material, either word-for-word or paraphrased, and often relate events in the same order. How did this happen? The scholarly consensus says Matthew and Luke knew Mark's Gospel and used it as one of their sources. Because Matthew and Luke share material not found in Mark, they also used another common source lost to us, dubbed Q after the German word for *source*. They also have unique materials, dubbed M and L respectively.[314] The synoptic Gospels are based on history and, if approached judiciously with scholarly tools, can disclose the historical Jesus.

The Gospel according to John is different. The synoptics portray Jesus' ministry lasting one year, John three. The synoptics have Jesus expel the moneychangers from the Temple just prior to his death, John early in his ministry. In the synoptics, the last supper is a Passover meal, in John it is not. John does not recount the transfiguration or the institution of the Eucharist, he relates neither exorcisms nor parables, and hardly mentions the kingdom of God, Jesus' constant subject in the synoptics. In John, Jesus teaches about himself. Because they are so different, both John and the synoptics cannot relate history. The scholarly consensus says John's Gospel is a product of the early church and, generously interpreted, reflects that church's experience of the risen Christ. The distinction between the synoptics and John is very old, made first by Clement of Alexandria (c.150-c.215) who comments on the spiritual nature of John's Gospel.

Partly because scholars solved the synoptic problem, scholarship has been able to distinguish the historical Jesus, the man who grew up in Nazareth whom the Romans crucified, from the early church's theology about him. Such a distinction is unknown to the seventeenth century and remains ignored by all the authors writing on Quakerism I have read, including contemporary ones. Yet, it is important, for it helps explain the split in nineteenth century

Quakerism and the battles fought in today's churches, both
Protestant and Catholic.

Wilmer Cooper highlights the distinction when he asks whether
salvation springs solely from the Light within or requires Jesus'
death.[315] He then proceeds to show how the early Quakers conflate several concepts:

> For Fox and early Friends the Holy Spirit was the resurrected
> Christ who is now present with us. He is not only the promised
> Counselor referred to by the Gospel of John (14:26) but is also
> identified with Jesus of the Synoptic Gospels, the incarnate Son
> of God who lived, taught, suffered, died, and rose again. He is
> the one who appeared at Pentecost.[316]

Cooper is right about the conflation. The early Quakers con-
founded three concepts: historical, doctrinal, and experiential.
History tells us a man, Jesus from Nazareth, was born into a Jewish
family in the homeland about 4 B.C.E. He grew up in Nazareth,
was baptized by John the Baptist, preached the kingdom of God,
attracted disciples, and upset the existing authorities. The Romans
crucified him near Jerusalem about 33 C.E. All this (and more)[317]
is history. Jesus' history ends with his crucifixion.

The figure who was born of a virgin, died for our sins, rose
bodily from the grave, and went to heaven where he stayed to return
someday, is a theological construct. The seventeenth century treats
it as history. So do conservative theologians today. However, it is
not history. History can tell us that people believed in virgin births
– the pagan world in Jesus' day believed in them, but Jews did not
– but not that they occur. History tells us Jesus died because he
frightened and/or angered the Temple and Roman authorities. It
can tell us Paul believed Jesus died for our sins to appease God's
wrath or satisfy God's justice, but it cannot claim Jesus did die for
that reason because history cannot ascertain the thoughts of God
or the gods.

History can tell us people believe in miracles, but it cannot
prove miracles occur. Jesus' bodily ascension, a miracle, was never
history. We now know it cannot have happened, even as miracle.
In Luke's day (the only Gospel to tell of the ascension), heaven
was a place above the solid, azure dome of the sky, so Jesus' ascension into it made sense. As noted, the seventeenth century
watched biblical cosmology collapse, and Milton struggles with its

disintegration in his great epic whose drama demands heaven and hell be places. Now we live with a cosmology that locates our sun in the starry heavens. Given modern cosmology, where would Jesus' body go? Jupiter? Andromeda? Ascending in a thinning and cooling atmosphere, it died again if it traveled far. The only people to solve the problem of bodily ascension while retaining modern cosmology claim Jesus' body was swept into a passing alien spacecraft. To say the least, such a claim requires some biblical, extrabiblical, and theological substantiation!

Finally, experience. The Logos, the eternal Christ who was present with people before Jesus' birth, became fully incarnate in Jesus, and is here now, is experiential. In Trinitarian theology, this is the Holy Spirit sweeping through the disciples at Pentecost. For Quakers, it is the Light within, with its many metaphoric designations. This is the deity as human beings experience it. More skeptically, the Logos/Light/Spirit serves as a metaphor for experiences people interpret in supernatural terms. In any case, this concept, although some people know it only from books or other people, secondhand, is based in many people's personal, firsthand experience.

The early Quakers simply conflate the three concepts.[318] Theologically, Quakers split in America in the nineteenth century when that conflation disintegrated. Quakers who wanted to appropriate Christian orthodoxy emphasized the theological concepts, atonement theology with its focus on Jesus' death, and the authority of the Bible. Quakers who tried to adhere to early Quaker beliefs retained experience as the primary authority and locus of salvation. Atonement theology, with its angry God who needs appeasement, did not fit well within a theology that emphasized spiritual experience, divinity within everyone, universal grace, and the possibility of universal salvation.

Without knowing our modern concept of the historical Jesus, early Quakerism used it, nonetheless. Quakers – we know most about Fox – tried to be him, to incarnate the Logos, the same Spirit Jesus incarnated in his life and teaching. Fox's life and that of the historical Jesus sketched by today's scholars are amazingly similar.[319] The nineteenth century split saw one side trying to incarnate Jesus, the other believing his death saves them. What the early Quakerism fused, the nineteenth century tore asunder.

Partly, the nineteenth century ruptured the synthesis because of the rise of critical New Testament scholarship, for that scholarship separates the historical Jesus of Nazareth from the theological figure, the Logos, the risen Christ. The historical Jesus, who was certainly a spiritually experienced man, fits well with the category of personal spiritual experience. Quaker belief is that the Spirit in/of Jesus, making him such a profound poet-teacher and enabling him to heal, is in everyone. Spiritualizing the theology as metaphor does not conflict with biblical scholarship. As metaphor, the theology says we are born of the Spirit (everyone has the Light within), the Light crucifies iniquity within us, and resurrects us as "new creation" (Gal. 6:15). The spiritual person is metaphorically Fox's Adam before the Fall and literally a purified being capable of living out the Quaker testimonies, producing fruits of the Spirit. In a virtuous circle, such a person follows the historical Jesus.

Problematic today is the treatment of theology as history. In orthodox salvation theology, Jesus died for our sins. In the Protestant version of salvation theology, he died in our place and God imputes his merit to the saved. This is Protestant substitution theology. Catholic theology offers a different explanation of Jesus' saving work: Jesus' death satisfies God's need for justice. This is Catholic satisfaction theology. These positions disagree with one another.

They also disagree with modern scholarship on the historical Jesus. One of the best-established historical facts about Jesus is that John the Baptist baptized him. In an extrabiblical work, the Jewish historian, Josephus, attests the historical existence of Jesus and John the Baptist.[320] All four Gospels – but only two biblical sources, Mark and John – tell of Jesus' baptism, although John avoids saying John the Baptist did the deed, and for good reason. John the Baptist's followers were rivals of Jesus' disciples, and John's baptism of Jesus was an embarrassment for the Jesus movement, for it makes John appear superior to Jesus. The Gospels recount the deed because the fact must have been so well known they could not avoid mentioning it and still claim to report history. However, they struggle to make Jesus superior to John. One of the best criteria for historicity is the recording of an event by people who would prefer not to record it, for they would hardly invent incidents harmful to their cause.

Judaism's sacred scriptures commanded sacrifice in the Temple for the forgiveness of sins. John baptized people in the Jordan for the forgiveness of their sins, ignoring or disobeying sacred scripture and the Temple authorities. Jesus forgave sins without sacrifice or baptism. He had difficulties with the Temple authorities whose livelihood depended on sacrifices continuing. At the last supper, he commented about having a different sacrifice from those made at the Temple, a non-bloody sacrifice of grain and grape.[321] In a word, Jesus did not believe God requires sacrifices, especially blood sacrifices, in order to forgive sins. Why, then, would he have deliberately gone to his bloody death as a sacrifice for sin? Orthodox sacrificial theology arises from St. Paul's (and others') efforts to explain and justify Jesus' crucifixion. It does not spring from Jesus.

Orthodox, sacrificial theology is also conceptually confused, failing the philosophical test of truth that it be logically coherent.[322] Justice is not satisfied when the innocent die in place of the guilty. A God who pretends sinners are righteous is dishonest, not good; one who saves and damns arbitrarily is unjust. Therefore, the theology is historically false by the standards of modern biblical scholarship, and philosophically false by the standards of coherence. Moreover, orthodoxy has two conflicting salvation theologies, Protestant and Catholic. Both cannot be true.

In contrast, early Quaker theology meshes nicely with historical Jesus scholarship. It downplays atonement theology. Indeed, it profits from its elimination because it spiritualizes the theology. Quakerism uses it as metaphor to speak of the spiritual life everyone may live, born of Spirit through the Light within, crucified from personal failings through repentance, and resurrected to new life in God here and now. Yet, while enervating the theology, early Quakers reinvigorate the historical Jesus. They seek to imitate him, and they believe doing so possible with the aid of the divine Light within that enabled Jesus to teach, heal, and live his simple lifestyle.

Thus, modern biblical scholarship undermines the two central poles of orthodox theology, the Fall and Jesus' death as a sacrifice for sin. In contrast, it streamlines and solidifies the core of early Quaker theology by demonstrating the distinction between history and theology. Core Quaker theology does not require an atonement, for its God is not angry. Nor does it insist the Bible be authoritative, for its God is within.

8. THE AUTHORITY OF SCRIPTURE

THE EARLY Quakers aim their arguments about scripture against the Protestants who believe scripture is inerrant and the primary authority in matters religious, historical, and scientific. They view Protestants as their principal theological foes, for rulers in England as long ago as Henry VIII (1491-1547) drove official Catholicism from England's shores. Quakerism arises in England when Protestantism is in the ascent. Barclay composes his *Catechism* to refute Protestantism's claims about scripture.

Barclay agrees with Protestants that the Bible offers the history of God's people, prophecy of past and future events, and doctrines concerning Christ. However, he rejects their claim that these are the Bible's main concerns. He sides with Protestantism against Catholicism on the two points about scripture separating them. Like Protestantism, he thinks Christian doctrines must be scriptural, and scripture is plain and easy to understand. Indeed, he argues throughout his *Catechism* that Quakerism fulfills these two criteria better than Protestantism does. He organizes his *Catechism* by propositions from Quaker theology followed by scriptural quotations supporting them.

This is early Quakerism. In the nineteenth century under Methodist influence, some people of Quaker background proclaimed the early Quakers wrong and embraced the primary authority of scripture and the centrality of the blood atonement.[323] Some of their followers today continue to call themselves Quakers. However, Barclay argues against these classical Protestant positions. This chapter presents his two main arguments about scripture, namely that it is not the primary authority but, nonetheless, Quakerism meets the Protestant criterion of explicating the plain meaning of scripture better than Protestantism does. Finally, the chapter demonstrates that modern biblical scholarship vindicates Barclay's opinion on scripture.

Quakerism and the text of scripture

Two examples from Barclay's *Catechism* of differences between Protestants and the early Quakers are especially clear. Protestants believe people remain sinful, even when saved, whereas Quakers believe God frees people from their sins, here and now. Protestants believe in the saving power of Christ on the cross alone, while the early Quakers believe in the saving power of Christ on the cross and within them. Chapter seven of Barclay's *Catechism* deals with the first issue.[324] Here I simplify it greatly.

Barclay asks, "May we then expect to be freed from the dominion of sin in this life?" and proceeds to offer the answer through scriptural quotations:

Rom. 6:14a. For sin will have no dominion over you.

Rom. 8:1-2. There is therefore now no condemnation for those who are in Christ Jesus . . . [who] has set you free from the law of sin and of death.

Rom. 8:35. Who will separate us from the love of Christ?

Rom. 6:15. What then? Should we sin because we are not under law but under grace? By no means!

Rom. 6:2-23. How can we who died to sin go on living in it? . . . We know that our old self was crucified with him so that the body of sin might be destroyed, and we might no longer be enslaved to sin. . . . You, having been set free from sin, have become slaves of righteousness. . . . But now that you have been freed from sin and enslaved to God, the advantage you get is sanctification.

Matt. 5:48. Be perfect, therefore, as your heavenly Father is perfect.

1 John 1:8-9. If we confess our sins, he who is faithful and just will forgive us our sins and cleanse us from all unrighteousness.

1 John 3:2-10. . . . No one who abides in him [Christ] sins. . . .

And so on. The power of Barclay's argument lies in its cumulative effect, as scriptural quotation after quotation flows from his pen. Moreover, he sharpens his argument by interlacing the quotations with questions omitted here for brevity. The original is worth consulting. An argument that marches so relentlessly is impressive. Contrary to classical Protestant doctrine, scripture plainly says Christ frees us from sin now, just as Quakerism claims.

In the same way, Barclay draws his readers to the efficacy of the Light within by the final question and answer[325] in chapter three on the significance of Christ. I quote in full:

Q. The scriptures cited generally indicate that the sufferings and death of Christ are effective for destroying, removing, and pardoning sins; did he accomplish this while outwardly on the earth, or did he leave something for himself to do in us, and for us to do in and by his strength?

A. 1 Pet. 2:21. For to this you have been called, because Christ also suffered for you, leaving you an example, so that you should follow in his steps. . . .

Col. 1:23-24. I, Paul, became a servant of this gospel. I am now rejoicing in my sufferings for your sake, and in my flesh I am completing what is lacking in Christ's afflictions for the sake of his body, that is, the church.

2 Cor. 4:10-11. . . . always carrying in the body the death of Jesus, so that the life of Jesus may also be made visible in our bodies. For while we live, we are always being given up to death for Jesus' sake, so that the life of Jesus may be made visible in our mortal flesh.

2 Cor. 5:15. And he died for all, so that those who live might live no longer for themselves, but for him who died and was raised for them.

Phil. 3:10. I want to know Christ and the power of his resurrection and the sharing of his sufferings by becoming like him in his death. . . .

More than one New Testament author clearly believes we have work to do, dying to our former selves and making Christ visible to others through our lives, imitating Jesus Christ through his power in us. The external work of Christ's atonement is conjoined in scripture with his internal transformation of those who follow him.

These brief examples from two chapters of Barclay's eighteen chapter *Catechism* refuting the main Protestant doctrines from scripture substantiate Barclay's argument that Quakerism follows scripture's plain sense better than Protestantism does. Nonetheless, he does not consider scripture the primary authority.

Quakerism and the authority of scripture

Barclay argues that scripture cannot be the primary authority because it fails to fit the appropriate criteria. Cooper summarizes Barclay's argument in four points.[326]

First, any primary directive must supply its own authority, but scripture does not. Rather, its authority springs from the Holy Spirit.

Second, for Christians any primary rule must differentiate between the law and the gospel. However, the New Testament, like the law in the Hebrew Scriptures, is external, a written text, so it does not differentiate between law and gospel. Only the gospel in the heart can do that.

Third, that which is primary must guide people in every situation, but the Bible does not. Rather, it offers general guidelines. People require the living presence of the Holy Spirit for personal tutoring and assurance of salvation.

Fourth, primary authorities must be accessible to everyone, but the Bible is not.

The first point carries enormous power because Christians of every sect and denomination agree that, in the final analysis, authority originates with the Holy Spirit. The Roman Catholic and Eastern Orthodox Churches (on slightly different grounds) claim the church is the primary authority, but when asked why, ultimately, they say because the Holy Spirit inspires it. Protestants declare the Bible the primary authority and, when asked why, say the Holy Spirit inspired it. Therefore, when Quakers assert the Holy Spirit is the primary authority, they speak for Christendom. Ecclesiastical and biblical authorities are derivative, secondary. The authority behind them is the divine Spirit speaking through them.

In a metaphor, Barclay refers to the Spirit or the Light as the Source. Scripture, he asserts, is not the Source, but merely declares the Source.[327] And again, Christendom must agree. God is the source of all. Going further, Fox claims the Light within judges the scripture: "And the light within, and the spirit of God within, that gave forth the scripture, is the trial of the scripture of truth."[328] He might have quoted Matthew 22:36-40 where Jesus, asked which is the greatest commandment, replies love to God and neighbor, then adds, "On these two commandments hang all the law and the prophets." Apparently, the law (Torah) and the prophets are to be judged as issuing from God only if they correspond with the commandment to love God and neighbor.

Both Fox and Barclay believe the Spirit necessary if a reader or hearer is to believe the scriptures or to understand them rightly.[329] In more than one writing, Fox observes that the Pharisees possessed the scriptures, but without the Spirit, they misinterpreted them.[330] Barclay reminds his readers that the written letter kills, only the Spirit gives life (2 Cor. 3:6).[331] He notes that the Gospel of John 5:39-40 shows Jesus castigating the Jews for valuing the scriptures too highly while ignoring him to whom the scriptures point.[332] Many Quaker writers comment that the scriptures cannot rescue people from sin. Only the Spirit saves.[333]

Finally, as Cooper observes, Barclay finds the Bible an insufficient guide for the individual. He refers to St. Paul's metaphor of the church as the body of Christ, with individuals having various functions, some as hands, some as eyes, some as feet (1 Cor. 12:12-31). However, scripture cannot tell individuals seeking guidance whether they are hands or feet.[334]

Finally, Barclay concludes that scripture is not mainly for teaching doctrine or behavior. Rather, it portrays the spiritual experiences of ancient people from which we can learn by analogy. It provides a kind of mirror that confirms our faith and strengthens our hope. We see God has protected others. The Spirit that moved the ancients provokes in us a response to their stories, for the same Spirit prods us. People in their natural state cannot interpret scripture properly, for that requires the activity of the same Spirit in the interpreter that acted in the lives portrayed.[335] Writing in the middle of the twentieth century, Quaker Henry Cadbury agrees. He considers the Bible a record of others' faith and virtue rather than a blueprint for faith and conduct.[336]

Another reason Barclay rejects the Bible as the primary authority is the scholarly challenge to its inerrancy. He argues the canon – the books considered sacred – is uncertain. The first centuries failed to agree on the documents to constitute sacred scripture.[337]

Moreover, the canon may be incomplete, for books now lost might be found and added to it.[338] Furthermore, adds Barclay, to proclaim scripture the only rule of faith, then request readers to have faith in a canon not listed in scripture is a mistake.[339] How do we prove, he asks, the Epistle of James authentic?[340] (Luther wanted to remove it from the canon.) Admittedly Revelation 22:18 warns the hearer not to add or subtract from the words of "the book of this prophecy." However, as Barclay notes, the words only apply to "this prophecy," not to the entire Bible. Moreover, such warnings appear in the Bible as early as Deuteronomy 4:2![341] Yet, most of the Bible was written since the events Deuteronomy narrates. As Cadbury notes, Quakers have never been impressed with the limits of the canon. Revelation is not limited to scripture.[342]

Even if the canon were certain, accurate textual transmission is not, Barclay argues. We lack the originals, and mistakes creep into hand-copied texts. Familiar with two textual traditions for the Hebrew Scriptures, the Hebrew version and the Greek translation of it whose beginnings date to before Jesus' time, Barclay asks, where they differ which should we trust?[343] He neglects to mention that Europe discovered a third textual tradition in 1616, published in England in 1657, the Samaritan Torah. It commands worship on Mt. Gerizim instead of Mt. Ebal (Deut. 27:4), a controversy between Samaritans and Judeans that lasted into the first centuries before the Common Era and continues in small pockets in the Middle East today. When compared, the texts confuse.

In contrast, the Holy Spirit speaks clearly, says Barclay. When illiterate people hear scripture, they occasionally judge some passages wrong. Upon checking the passages, Barclay found them corrupted.[344] He is not alone. A modern book has the audacity to demonstrate that orthodox Christians altered passages in the New Testament to fit orthodox ideology.[345]

Moreover, most people must read the Bible in translation, but observes Barclay, "Even the latest translations require many corrections and amendments."[346] Barclay must have known several English translations, for portions of the Bible appear in English as early as the tenth century, and the whole Bible appears before Barclay's time under the names of Wycliffe (1390s), Tyndale (1526-35), Coverdale (1535), Matthew's Bible (1537), the Geneva Bible (1557), and the Bishops' Bible (1568). By Barclay's day, the King James Version (1611) had superseded the others, but it was only the latest. Some of the translations differed substantially. Renowned for its beauty, the King James Version served as the Bible of the early Quakers and most English-speaking Christians into modern times, but based as it is on late manuscripts and insufficient knowledge of the biblical languages, it contains many errors. Modern biblical criticism discloses these and other problems.

Modern biblical criticism

Modern biblical criticism substantiates Barclay's arguments while adding important details and fresh knowledge. For example, increased knowledge renders the canon even more uncertain than Barclay thought. The early church collected Paul's letters by its crucial criterion for inclusion in the canon: an apostle (Paul) wrote them. Scholars are now sure Paul is not the author of at least four of the thirteen letters, and two others are of questionable authorship. Thus, almost half the Pauline corpus may be inauthentic. Should these letters remain in the canon when they fail the essential criterion of inclusion? Moreover, the canon of the Hebrew Scriptures differs from church to church. The Catholic Church, Protestant Churches, and the Eastern Orthodox Churches recognize different scriptures as canonical although, of course, the contents overlap considerably. However, for its Old Testament, the Eastern Church uses the Septuagint, the ancient Greek translation. The Septuagint was the Bible of the early church and therefore constitutes the founding text of Christianity. Nonetheless, Protestants and Catholics reject it in favor of the Hebrew text Jews use. In scholarly terms, this is the Massoretic text of the Leningrad Codex.[347] In places, it differs substantially from the Septuagint.

Until the discovery of the Dead Sea Scrolls in 1947, the differences might be credited to translation. However, among the Dead Sea Scrolls are fragments, and sometimes complete scrolls, of every book in the Hebrew Scriptures except Esther. All the copies date to before the Common Era. Often, more than one copy of a book survives. Some copies closely resemble the Massoretic text, but others mirror the Septuagint. Still others reflect neither. Not only was there no established canon before the common era, there was no authenticated text. What, then, set the canon and canonical text? History is uncertain. Moreover, the discovery of the Gospel of Thomas at Nag Hammadi, Egypt, in 1945, with its one hundred fourteen sayings, many similar to the sayings in the synoptics, has led some scholars to propose opening the canon of the Bible to new discoveries – just as Barclay suggested might happen.

Since the mid-nineteenth century, a flood of new manuscripts has been discovered. As a result, scholars now possess thirty-four different Gospels[348] and more than five thousand Greek manuscripts of the New Testament, although some are very fragmentary. No copies, except very small fragments, agree in exact wording. The differences are literally countless – there are more than there are words in the New Testament.[349] In order to develop a single text of the New Testament, scholars use these, plus earlier scholarly editions, to produce the best text possible. Therefore, the best modern Greek text of the New Testament is a scholarly compilation from thousands of manuscripts, none dating to earlier than one hundred seventy-five years after the death of Jesus. Such a process and time gap guarantee the best modern reconstruction of the text differs from the original.

Even so, the King James Version developed in distressing contrast. It rests on a Greek text extracted from a few late manuscripts and a Greek edition Erasmus developed in 1516 that sports some unfounded conjectures in the text. Barclay was correct: even the best Greek text of his time contained major errors.

He was also right about translations. All anyone need do is compare our plethora of English translations to one another to know they differ. The New Revised Standard Version preferred by most scholars for its inclusive language sometimes mauls Paul's meaning. For example, in Galatians 4:1-7, Paul writes to his converts in the NRSV: "My point is this: heirs, as long as they are minors, are no better than slaves. . . . But . . . God sent his son . . . so that we might receive adoption as children. . . . So you are no longer a slave but a child." This translation makes no sense. Children are no better than slaves, so you are not a slave but a child? Paul intends to discuss a radical change in status. His point is, you are no longer slaves, but sons and heirs. How much better, then, the original exclusive language reads: "God sent his son . . . so that we might receive sonship. . . . So you are no longer a slave, but a son."[350] Not only does it capture the altered status, but also the son-son repetition makes Christ God's son and the converts, likewise, God's sons. This translation, so close to the original, shows us where in scripture Fox gleaned the idea that those responsive to the Light within resemble Christ and, like him, may be perfect, free from sin.

Modern scholars, of course, are more skeptical of the Bible than anyone was in seventeenth century Christendom. They know more. Science has found the Earth round, our sun one of a myriad stars, life a product of natural selection over several billion years, and our universe ancient, indeed. History has turned much of the Hebrew Scriptures into legend, undermining events even as late as the Exodus, the conquest, the monarchy of David and Solomon, and, of course, the Mosaic authorship of the first five biblical books. As scholars have discovered, the Hebrew Scriptures and the New Testament reflect their authors' and editors' theological and political agendas. As the early Quakers never tired of repeating, they do not convey the words of God. The Quakers added: Christ is God's Word. Look to the Light within.

Modern scholarship agrees with the early Quakers on several more points about scripture. Fox thought the era of law ended. Modern scholarship believes Paul thought the same. Quakers emphasize transformation and the Spirit within. Paul and the early church emphasize them, too, says modern scholarship. Quakers stress spiritual resurrection, turning Jesus' possible bodily resurrection into a metaphor.[351] Modern scholarship notes Paul's treatment of Jesus' resurrection is spiritual, not physical.

The most skeptical scholars claim divine inspiration is a fable, therefore nothing is inspired. Those less skeptical believe inspiration does happen but, therefore, in addition to the Bible much extrabiblical literature is inspired, also. Perhaps, for example, Shakespeare's ringing poetry, Milton's great epic and/or the Chinese religious classic, the *Tao Te Ching* are all inspired. In either case, the Bible no longer stands alone as the one inspired work of God.

Furthermore, modern biblical scholarship undermines the belief that major Christian doctrines can be validly derived from the Bible. The Fall, of course, has gone. But also the Trinity, already rejected by the early Quakers, comes from Greek philosophy, not the Bible. As long ago as the eighteenth century, an Anglican theologian, William Whiston (1667-1752),[352] read the New Testament thoroughly hoping to prove the orthodox doctrine scriptural. He concluded, instead, that the New Testament supports Arianism, heresy to Trinitarians.

Scholarship refutes the five fundamentals of Christian fundamentalism. It shows the Bible ambiguous about Jesus' bodily resurrection – so were the early Quakers. It disproves verbal inerrancy – the early Quakers disbelieved biblical inerrancy, too. It rejects the substitutionary atonement – the early Quakers spiritualized it nearly into non-existence. Scholarship undermines the virgin birth[353] (and science shows it impossible by modern biological understandings of DNA and conception) – Fox spiritualized it. And, finally, modern biblical scholarship places the question of Jesus' divinity beyond historical reach because it cannot be ascertained by historical methods. Here, scholarship and early Quakerism differ. The early Quakers believed Jesus divine. However, in opposition to the Protestants, they appropriated his divinity in their lives rather than receiving it as a proposition accepted on faith.

Modern scholarship renders the truth of the Bible far more uncertain than it was in Barclay's day and the biblical basis of fundamental Christian doctrines deeply questionable if not false. Such scholarly skepticism alters the balance between the authority of the Light within and the Bible. Barclay fought hard in his *Catechism* and *Apology* to diminish the authority of the Bible upheld by the best Protestant scholars of his day. Now, scholarship takes Barclay's side. Scholarly criticism of the Bible renders the Light within relatively stronger as a source of authority. Fox, deeply moved by both, perhaps states the Quaker position best. The gospel to be preached, he claims, is God's love.[354] The gospel is neither words nor propositions but power – the power of God.[355] The cross is the power of God.[356] He cites from the Bible example after example of heathens inspired by the Spirit and concludes that we do not need to depend on scripture to know God. He especially likes Peter's comment to the pagan Cornelius: "'I truly understand that God shows no partiality, but in every nation anyone who fears him and does what is right is acceptable to him'" (Acts 10:34-35).[357] He tells illiterate people scripture resides within them. Therefore, they should be unconcerned about their inability to read the outward words.[358]

Modern biblical scholarship shows the Quakers right from the first. Scripture is not the primary authority. Indeed, modern biblical scholarship shreds its inerrancy. In contrast, the Light within stands untouched by biblical scholarship, history, or science.[359] Therefore, since the seventeenth century its authority has risen relative to the Bible. Throughout this book thus far, I have assumed the Light is universal. The early Quakers offer reasons to think it so.

9. UNIVERSALISM

CHRISTIAN THEOLOGY allows two types of universalism. Some Christian groups maintain salvation is universal. In the end, God saves everyone. The early Quakers embrace a different universalist claim. They assert God imbues everyone, without exception, with divine Light. George Fox declares, "God hath given to every one of you a measure of his spirit according to your capacities; liars, drunkards, whoremongers, and thieves, and who follow filthy pleasures, you all have this measure in you."[360] Jim Pym, writing today, notes that this Light within everyone has many names: That of God, the Mind in Christ, the Cosmic Christ, the unborn Buddha Mind, the Original Face, Atman, Tao, Soul, and Spirit.[361] Quaker universalists believe everyone has the Light. No religious tradition has a monopoly on it.[362] Contemporary theologian, John Hick, suggests it is time to remove particular religions from the center of faith and, instead, concentrate our attention on God who, after all, is the reality behind every faith.[363]

The early Quakers offer four arguments for the universality of the Light. One is logical, based on the Christian salvation story. Another is minutely scriptural, heaping up biblical quotations as proofs. A third depends on experience, both inner, subjective encounters of one's own and narratives by others coupled with their objectively observable actions. A fourth claims the universality of the Light exalts God's graciousness.

The early Quakers also present negative arguments. They attempt to demonstrate orthodoxy is illogical, unscriptural, narrowly intellectual, and injurious to Christianity's image of a good God. To understand their position requires a brief excursion into orthodoxy.

Orthodoxy

Protestant orthodoxy borrows from Augustine the doctrine of predestination. Simplified, the doctrine affirms that because of the

Fall, all people are corrupted, condemned, and deserve damnation. However, God in mercy sends Jesus to die as a substitute for some sinners, those to whom God imputes grace. They stay corrupt but, nonetheless, God saves them. God damns the remainder to endless punishment. Individuals can do nothing to change their status, for God predestines their salvation or damnation from all eternity.[364]

Barclay pronounces the doctrine "horrible and blasphemous."[365] As he observes, despite clever arguments attempting to avoid its logic, the doctrine makes God the author of sin. Indeed, he quotes Calvin who explicitly says God ordained and willed Adam's fall. There is no doubt who is responsible for sin here![366]

Barclay comments also that the doctrine warps Christ's incarnation and death, turning them "into a testimony of God's wrath to the world."[367] It also renders all preaching useless, for human preaching cannot change eternal, divine decrees. Indeed, according to the doctrine of predestination, says Barclay, people suffer more for less reason than do the devils in hell. The devils endure the torments of hell only because of their own deeds, and then only for a time, whereas the doctrine of predestination hurls people into hell forever for someone else's sin.[368]

The Catholic Church, Barclay remarks, goes to the other extreme, making its own actions efficacious for salvation, although those who participate in them may remain sinners. The sacraments convey grace, whether the officiant or recipient is worthy or not. Indeed, people can purchase grace through pilgrimages, masses, and other ceremonies.[369] Under neither version of orthodoxy do people need to change, to be transformed into holy beings,[370] although Catholicism holds such transformation possible and important.

The orthodox Christian position, then, despite the wide differences between Catholicism and Protestantism, holds Jesus' sacrifice all-sufficient, separates grace from holiness, and retains our sinful state, even in the saved.[371] For Catholicism, the church with its sacraments, pilgrimages, and indulgences mediates divine grace. Protestantism rejects any mediation but Christ's. Because the merits of Jesus' death are not universally available, the one universal in Christian orthodoxy is sin. Early Quakerism insists on another universal, the Light within.

Quakerism

Quakerism offers four arguments for the universality of the Light within. The order given here is arbitrary. Easiest to follow is the logic of salvation.

Quakerism agrees with orthodoxy, following St. Paul, that all sin in Adam. But Paul balances his "all die in Adam" with "so all will be made alive in Christ" (1 Cor. 15:22). Jesus is the second Adam. He reverses the effects of the first. If all are cursed in Adam, all are blessed in Christ. "This light [Christ]" Barclay asserts, "is no less universal than the seed of sin, being purchased by his death who tasted death for everyone."[372] He then quotes 1 Corinthians 15:22 and, later, Romans 5:18: "Therefore just as one man's trespass led to condemnation for all, so one man's act of righteousness leads to justification and life for all."[373] There is logical symmetry here. If in Adam all die, in Christ all live.

Barclay continues the logic of his (and Paul's) argument: "Certainly, if those who have never heard of Adam are injured by his fall through the seed of evil that lies within them, why can't they be saved by the gift and grace of Christ in them?"[374] He comments that God accepted Cornelius, a pagan Roman, and sent Peter to him. Cornelius feared God without knowledge of the gospel or of Jesus' life and death. Surely, God also reaches others who know neither the gospel nor the historical Jesus.[375]

Christians writing in defense of Christianity in the second and third centuries agreed. They viewed other religions and their adherents positively because they believed the divine Word universally present. Thus, it manifest itself in other religions, not only paganism and Judaism, but Buddhism and Hinduism.

Nonetheless, the universality of the Light does not imply that salvation is universal. Although everyone has the seed of grace within, not everyone responds to it. The Light is universal; God's offer of salvation is universal; but because some resist and reject the divine Light, neither enlightenment nor salvation is universal. That is the sum and substance of the early Quaker doctrine of universalism. The symmetric logic of salvation makes it available to all – all have the Light within. Nonetheless, not all are saved, not because of God's eternal decree, but through human defiance, here and now.

This view of Christian doctrine exalts God's grace, explains Barclay, as he begins his second argument for the universality of the Light. Under the Quaker conception of Christian theology, God provides all good, whereas we condemn ourselves.

As Barclay elucidates the Quaker position, people in their natural state who remain unaware of the Light within cannot initiate their own salvation. Rather, the divine Light in people first enlightens them. If they respond favorably to its initiative, they can continue to cooperate with it until it transforms what is natural by what is divine. Thus, God saves us. Although we may cooperate in our own salvation, we do not save ourselves.

On the other hand, people condemn themselves. God moves them, shines divine Light within them, but they ignore the movement, shield their eyes from the Light. God wrestles with them, but they refuse submission. Stubbornly egocentric, they stand condemned.

The doctrine of the universal seed also exalts Christ's death, proclaims Barclay, for his sacrifice is sufficient to save everyone. Moreover, because Christ is within people, the doctrine brings salvation closer than breath.[376]

For his third argument, Barclay demonstrates that scripture speaks of the Light as universal. He quotes John 1:9: "'The true light, which enlightens everyone, was coming into the world.'" He calls it "the Quaker text,"[377] for John so clearly declares the Light enlightens everyone that elaborate interpretation is unnecessary. Barclay goes on to quote Micah, Romans, Hebrews, and Jeremiah[378] who deliver the same message. Furthermore, his *Catechism* confirms the scriptural support for the universality of the Light, as it propounds one quotation after another. Because the text is readily available and this method of argument is relatively obsolete today, the quotations are not cited here. However, as in the *Apology*, they abound and derive from the Hebrew Scriptures as well as the New Testament.

The fourth argument relies on experience. It has two facets. First is the argument from personal, subjective experience, and second from personal, objective experience – from experience recorded in history and/or noted in behavior.

Barclay handles the argument from experience gingerly. He grants Quakers experience God's grace, seed, or Light, but admits people lacking such experiences have difficulty grasping them intellectually.[379] Indeed, some consider Quakers "fools and madmen."[380] Barclay urges patience and practice. He suggests people lay aside speculative and learned arguments, cease speaking, and wait in silence. Then, if they attend to the Light, they will discover a two-edged sword cutting away those things natural to people and making them "tremble and become Quakers indeed."[381] Finally, he quotes scripture in warning: "'Examine yourselves to see whether you are living in the faith. Test yourselves. Do you not realize that Jesus Christ is in you? – unless, indeed, you fail to meet the test!'" (2 Cor. 13:5).

The test is simple: "As the inward and substantial seed in our hearts is nourished and grows we become capable of tasting, smelling, seeing, and handling the things of God, for these things are beyond our ordinary spirit and sense."[382] Those who heed the seed within come to know God experientially. Barclay himself experienced God's presence as "a secret power" he yielded to and felt "the evil in me weakening, and the good lifted up."[383]

Fox, a person of visionary spiritual sensibility, perceives the universality of the Light inwardly.

> For I saw that Christ had died for all men, and was a propitiation for all, and had enlightened all men and women with his divine and saving light, and that none could be a true believer but who believed it. I saw that the grace of God, which brings salvation, had appeared to all men, and that the manifestation of the Spirit of God was given to every man to profit withal. These things I did not see by the help of man, nor by the letter, though they are written in the letter, but I saw them in the light of the Lord Jesus Christ, and by his immediate Spirit and power, as did the holy men of God, by whom the Holy Scriptures were written.[384]

Fox believes the universality of the Light, the universality of the indwelling Christ, because his direct experience reveals it. He has no need of scripture to discover it, although scripture tells of it, too.

Barclay argues the second facet as well, the personal experience known objectively by observers because they can perceive virtuous actions and ideas. He discusses the righteousness of Job and the wisdom of the pagan philosophers, much debated in the seventeenth century because so obviously ethical, yet lacking biblical revelation. He even mentions an Arabic book that recounts how one Hai Eben Yokdan came to know God so intimately he discoursed with the divine.[385] None of these people knows about Jesus. Here is evidence from scripture, philosophy, and history that people outside the Christian fold live righteous lives and know God. Such examples constitute further evidence that the Light dwells in everyone and God is no respecter of persons or religions.

Modern biblical criticism obviates the soundness of some of these arguments, but it injures the orthodox far more than it harms the early Quakers.

Modern biblical criticism

Modern biblical criticism destroys two of the major arguments. First, it ruins the logic of the argument from scripture shared in part by the orthodox and the Quakers. Without Eve, Adam, and the Fall, the logic of Christ as second Adam, undoing the consequences of Adam and Eve's misdeed, disintegrates. The results for orthodoxy have been discussed and need no repetition. The full effects on Quakerism appear in chapters eleven and twelve. Here, suffice it to say that the logical symmetry of Barclay's theology that all sinned in Adam, so all are enlightened by Christ, loses its equilibrium. If a similarly symmetric argument is to succeed in establishing the universality of the Light, it requires new grounding.

Because biblical criticism undermines the authority of the Bible, the method of argument of piling scriptural quotations one upon the other to prove a point becomes anachronistic. If scripture is no longer authoritative, a stack of quotations from it proves only that it favors that point, not that the point is correct. Thus, even if Quakers do win the argument by this method as Barclay proclaims, they triumph only in the seventeenth century, not today.

However, modern biblical criticism leaves untouched the other Quaker arguments for the presence of the divine seed in everyone. Nonetheless, in reviewing them, it is important to tread carefully. The weakness of the argument from subjective experience is well known. Not everyone has such experiences. Moreover, such experiences may arise from unbalanced minds or suffer misconstrual. In addition, people interpret such experiences within the framework of their own cultures, so whether one hears or perceives

Gabriel, Christ, Buddha, Krishna, or Moroni is culturally conditioned.

However, the Quaker argument reaches beyond such experiences to center on their results. Are people changed inwardly? Do they begin to live lives filled with the fruit of good works, replete with love of God and neighbor? These are objective standards, captured in the Quaker testimonies of peace, equality, simplicity, truth telling, and community. As another believer in the universal Light, William Penn, notes, "'The humble, meek, merciful, just, pious, and devout souls of the world are everywhere of one religion.'"[386]

Moreover, the argument draws strength from humility. If I claim to have the divine Light dwelling in me, humility demands I believe the same of others. To declare I have a spark of the divine, but you do not, struts sheer arrogance. Fox and Barclay readily agree that some respond better than others do, for some indulge in "filthy pleasures," whereas others visit the imprisoned, clothe the naked, feed the hungry, and care for the sick (Matt. 25:35-36). But Fox and Barclay never arrogantly claim the divine exclusively for themselves and/or their coterie.

The objective argument from historical experience survives, too. Job, the pagan philosophers, and other non-Christians exhibit closeness to God and live righteously. Fox writes of the Holy Spirit in Turks, Moors, and Indians.[387] Brinton notes similarities with other religions.[388] He comments that mysticism, attainment of "immediate and direct contact with the Divine, resulting in eventual union with God, occurs in all the great religions." He mentions the Sufi movement in Islam, Taoism in China, several branches of Hinduism and Zen Buddhism.[389] As Douglas Gwyn notes, Fox's claim that people can respond to the gospel inwardly without knowing it outwardly was revolutionary.[390] Among most Christians, it remains revolutionary today.

Biblical criticism also fails to shake the contention that the Quaker position exalts God's grace. As noted, early Quaker theology solves the problem of the creator's responsibility for the evil in humanity, a matter explored from a scientific viewpoint in chapter twelve. Moreover, it touches upon an important current discussion in philosophy of science and religion about the sphere of God's activity in the universe science describes: how to account for God's activity in the world without divine breach of natural laws, implying a kind of divine coercion. According to early Quakerism, the divine in humanity works to effect human transformation, but remains resistible. Hence, God transforms but never coerces.

These issues move beyond the subject of this chapter. This chapter addresses universalism in its early Quaker definition, that there is that of God in everyone – a radical inclusiveness. In contrast, orthodoxy excludes. Roman Catholicism claims its own institutional domain to be the kingdom of God,[391] with those outside its realm excluded from salvation. Protestantism demands knowledge of Jesus Christ's saving death on the cross and faith in it, which only some know about and fewer possess. Both depend on the Bible whose authority modern biblical criticism undermines. For example, Catholicism establishes its institutional claims on a passage in Matthew that recounts Peter's confession of Jesus as Messiah and Jesus' reply, "You are Peter [*rock* in Greek], and on this rock will I build my church . . . whatever you bind on earth will be bound in heaven, and whatever you loose on earth will be loosed in heaven" (Matt. 16:18-19).

Modern biblical criticism mistrusts Gospel passages that spring from only one source. This saying is solely in Matthew. Moreover, it clearly elaborates its source, Mark, who records only the confession, not Jesus' alleged reply. Furthermore, the Jesus Seminar, a collaboration of biblical scholars who labored together diligently over the question of which sayings attributed to Jesus go back to him, rates this saying as definitely not from Jesus. It is, rather, an invention of the early church, a confession of and model for its faith.[392] Crumbled, now, is the biblical foundation of the Catholic Church's assertion of exclusivity. It was built on a false attribution.

Protestantism claims to depend for its theology solely on the Bible. With the Bible's authority undermined, Protestant doctrines regarding the knowledge necessary for faith and divine acceptance disintegrate.

In contrast, although early Quakerism certainly reveres the Bible and believes it true, it does not depend on scripture for its foundation. Rather, Quakerism erects its theological edifice on the inner Light. Quakerism has faith that the Light resides in everyone. Its faith has arguments behind it that biblical criticism leaves untouched. People experience the Light (in diverse, metaphoric ways). The experience(s) transforms their lives into ones filled with love and care for others and love for God. Humility demands that, if I claim the Light is in me, I make the same claim for you. Moreover, much evidence exists that non-Christian lives are likewise transformed. Furthermore, such a belief glorifies God, which every Christian denomination believes incumbent upon us all. It seems logical, then, as well as experiential, that everyone has a glimmer of the Light within and those transformed radiate divine luminosity upon others.

The theology of the universality of the Light has further arguments in its favor. These develop with the rise of science, when Quakerism encounters new empirical knowledge.

SUMMARY OF THE CHALLENGE OF SCRIPTURE

Early Quakerism believes scripture recounts history, but nonetheless views scripture as primarily offering spiritual truths. Thus, the early Quakers believe Adam and Eve are historical figures and Jesus' atoning sacrifice really saves us. The conclusion they draw, however, differs radically from that of orthodox Christianity. Since Christ saves us, they think, he restores to humanity the possibility of the innocence of Adam and Eve before the Fall – a perfectly logical conclusion. Thus, when modern biblical criticism undermines the historicity and seamlessness of biblical narratives, Quaker theology remains unshaken because it depends on the spirituality of the Bible, not its literal truth.

Moreover, early Quakerism considers the Bible fallible. Barclay insists that the canon may be incomplete, knows Christians do not possess the original documents, and recognizes the difficulties inherent in translation. Thus, when modern biblical criticism finds errors in the Bible, Quakerism is unsurprised. When archaeologists discover lost manuscripts of very ancient texts, Barclay anticipates their discoveries. When new manuscripts and translations correct former errors, old Quakerism nods sagaciously. The Holy Spirit is the authority in early Quakerism, not the text of scripture or a particular translation of it or even the traditional canon.

Indeed, because early Quakerism considers the Light universal, it recognizes that people need not know the Bible at all to live righteous, humble, and peaceful lives. All people have the Light, and all can heed it – although all can also resist it. Nonetheless, early Quakerism thought salvation possible for everyone. By undermining the authority of the Bible and, with it, Christian orthodoxy, modern biblical criticism strengthens a Quakerism whose authority lies within.

PART III

SCIENCE: THE ENCOUNTER
WITH EMPIRICAL KNOWLEDGE

NICHOLAS Copernicus's *De Revolutionibus Orbium Caelestium* of 1543 placed the sun at the center of the universe and cast Earth out to become one of the planets revolving around it. The year 1543, then, provides a convenient date to mark the beginning of modern science. As soon as Galileo Galilei popularized the idea in the early 1600s, the Catholic Church placed Copernicus' book on its Index of prohibited books, allowing neither possession nor perusal. To locate the sun rather than the Earth at the center of the universe undermined the centrality of salvation theology and was contrary to the Bible and, therefore, heresy. Thus, almost at its inception, empirical science clashed with religious authority, the authority of church and scripture.

From ancient times, the wisdom of the past and its authority ruled the human mind. With the rise of science, experience began to test former truths, and new knowledge threatened past certainties. The development of radical religious sects such as the Quakers, with their emphasis on the immediacy of Spirit and personal encounter with it, absorbed the philosophy of experimental science and applied it to religion.[393] As related earlier, when George Fox challenged a Jesuit to perform an experiment to test Catholic claims concerning the Eucharist, Fox sided with experience against authority.

However, he could never have anticipated where experience would lead. Science now relates a coherent saga stretching from the origin of our universe in the big bang 13.7 billion years ago through the creation of the heavy chemical elements in the stars, to the formation of Earth some 4.6 billion years ago, to the evolution of species, including our own.

Before the twentieth century, science developed the metaphor of a grandfather clock to describe the universe. The universe resembled a big machine and matter appeared particulate, hard, indivisible, passive, separable from the observer, and completely

102

knowable. In contrast, the Spirit that Quakers claimed to encounter in their Meetings was ineffable, active, and mist-like, never fully knowable, a penetrable and penetrating radiance encountered within people. Matter and Spirit seemed worlds apart.

However, the rise of quantum mechanics and the proven equivalency of matter and energy in the twentieth century transformed science's concept of matter. Matter is a form of energy. It is ineffable, active, foamy, not fully knowable, and influenced by the observer. Thus, modern matter resembles Spirit. As Brinton notes, modern science fits spirituality far better than the older, mechanistic science.[394] It posits a creative universe in which, as biochemist and theologian Arthur Peacocke notes, "God does not make things, but makes things make themselves."[395]

Could the exploration of matter and Spirit be methodologically similar, too? Perhaps, but no method overarching all the sciences exists except in the very abstract. This is partly because method is difficult to describe exactly, but also because science's subjects are so diverse. Physics studies tiny entities outside ordinary experience, the atoms and their constituents. It uses instruments such as cyclotrons. Chemistry uses devices such as the centrifuge to study molecules. Astronomy investigates huge conglomerates like stars, galaxies, and the universe. It depends on telescopes to capture various sorts of radiation. Biology stretches from biochemistry to ecosystems to planetary phenomena and uses equipment as simple as binoculars and as complex as non-invasive scanning devises with their familiar acronyms – PET, CAT, MRI, and fMRI. Each pursuit requires its own special training and set of skills.

Science and religion author, Ken Wilber, suggests an abstract methodology to cover the sciences and religion, too. It begins with the injunction, "do this," whether the doing consists of looking through a telescope or mixing chemicals. Then the doer has direct, immediate experience, whether seeing a star or watching a liquid change color. Last comes communal confirmation or rejection by those who do the first two steps well.[396] This abstract, three-step description seems to capture how experimental science works. It also describes the steps involved in experiencing the spiritual realm, where "do this" might constitute "turn inward in silence," followed by direct, personal experience, and then by communal confirmation or rejection. Yet, the method is not so broad as to encompass any activity at all. It fails to describe learning from books or lectures or engaging in mathematics, for example, for all lack the experiential feature. So its congruence across experimental science and spirituality is suggestive.

The third part of this book explores the harmony or discord between science and Quakerism and between science and Christian orthodoxy, again considering Protestantism and Catholicism together. Wilber, whose work inspired me to write this book, offers many worthwhile suggestions about integrating science and religion.[397] Calvin Schwabe's pamphlet[398] lists attributes Quakerism and science share. The following chapter of this book, chapter ten, compares the attributes of science, Quakerism, and orthodoxy. Chapters eleven and twelve present science's saga and ask whether Quakerism and/or orthodoxy are compatible with it. The final chapter collects the diverse strands running through the book for a summary. But first, science needs illuminating.

10. SCIENCE IN THE LIGHT

NO DOUBT science and religion differ. Indeed, they often clash. Stephen Jay Gould argues that their foci are so dissimilar they heed non-overlapping magisteria and may live side by side without perturbation.[399] He is partly correct. Science is interested in the material world, its origin, development, constituents, and processes. Religion concentrates on the divine, salvation, the world beyond death, and living here and now in correspondence with the divine, whether conceived of as the Tao, the Buddha-nature, the will of Allah, the Holy Spirit, or the Light within. The question addressed here is not the broad one of how alike or different science and religion are, but a much narrower one, whether Christian orthodoxy or early Quakerism fits best with science. To find out, the attributes of science require elucidation.

Attributes of science

Experience is science's foundation. Science depends on experiment and observation, but also on the long-term experience of scientists, who must acquire a knack for their area of expertise. We know experience is primary because, if experiment or observation differs from theory, theoreticians return to the drawing board. Experience is, so to speak, the outside of science, its exteriority.

Its interiority is reason. Reason, resting (typically) on mathematical calculation, is science's architect. Without it, experience would collect data only to toss them into the basement. Reason organizes the data, or they would be useless and, moreover, overwhelm our capacity to think about them. Reason erects the superstructure, getting the rooms, windows, and doors in the right places and keeping them in square. Science's building is incomplete, but its foundation is firm, its walls are up, its roof on. We know its shape and many of its exits and entrances, even if, here and there, the scaffolding remains in place.

So, experience and reason are central. But they are not alone. Science also employs intuition, especially in the process of discovery. Science historians tell many discovery stories. One involves Charles Townes, the Nobel Prize-winning inventor of the laser.[400] In 1951, he sat on a committee convened to create better radar. The goal proved elusive. The morning before the last meeting, resting quietly on a park bench because he had awakened before his hotel's café opened, illumination came, and within minutes he solved the conundrum of how to produce stronger microwaves, the same principle later applied to both the maser and laser. He compares his experience to the enlightenment of the Buddha or Moses' revelation at the burning bush. His discovery was not a rational process, but came as if by revelation. Many scientific discoveries arrive in similar fashion, intuitively.

If chasing wealth and sensual experience is worldly, science is unworldly. Although it requires funding, its heart is not on the bottom line. Rather, it concentrates on nature, whether stars, electrons, or fruit flies. Fundamental science does not even concern itself with its usefulness in the world. It seeks knowledge for its own sake, just to know. Typically, science reaches beyond the ordinary senses, forsaking appearances for a deeper reality.

Yet, science carries its new discoveries back to the world, hoping to improve it. Townes particularly rejoices in the laser's usefulness in eye surgery, enabling those with dimming sight to see clearly again.

Science is communal. Most scientists today work in teams, and many scientific papers bear the names of multiple authors. Moreover, scientists check each other's work, not only by appraising articles submitted to journals, but also by repeating others' observations and experiments to see whether the same results appear.

Science rejects authority. Nonetheless, it learns from the past. Isaac Newton famously commented, "If I have seen farther, it is because I have stood on the shoulders of giants."[401] Furthermore, scientists respect excellence. Nobel Prize-winners carry weight. Yet, nothing freezes. Today can improve on the past; Nobel laureates, too, make mistakes. So, science is poised between respecting the past rather than forever beginning anew, yet reviewing and overturning the past when anomalies arise that question past insights.

Science seeks truth. It finds an odd kind of truth, though, a changing one. Nonetheless, the change is neither arbitrary nor irrational. Scientific truth changes because science assimilates new facts. It may know A, B, and C but, with current theory, be unable to integrate D or E. Then, a new theory arises that integrates A, B, C, D, and E while unexpectedly encompassing F and G and suggesting new discoveries at H and I. Philosophers of science speak of this process as "consilience," a bringing together of previously disparate fields of knowledge, fitting new pieces into the puzzle, constructing another room in the building, filling in the narrative.

Apprenticeship is required. Perhaps it commences with a high school science project, begun as a sophomore and awarded three years later. It continues into a four-year undergraduate degree, three, four, or five years to a doctorate, then a post-doctorate position lasting another year or two or three. In round numbers, a dozen years of study are required before the scientific community accepts a new scientist into its membership.

During these years, budding scientists acquire certain virtues. They learn patience, undoubtedly, but also honesty, for the whole community suffers if a scientist fudges the books, so the community demands honesty. Humility is valued, too. Thomas Huxley, the great nineteenth century biologist known as Darwin's bulldog, writes, "'Sit down before fact as a little child, be prepared to give up every preconceived notion, follow humbly and to whatever abysses Nature leads, or you shall learn nothing.'"[402] Attentiveness is necessary, long hours of concentration. Scientists must be curious, truth-seeking and –telling people. They must cooperate, learn to work on a team. And, finally, peace is necessary. The ideal is rational discussion and careful experiment/observation. Scientists try to convince each other. They do not duel with what George Fox calls "carnal weapons," but with reason and evidence.

These are virtues the scientist develops as scientist, the ones the profession demands. The virtues may, or may not, carry over into the scientist's other pursuits. Scientists, as human beings, can be egocentric, arrogant, and dishonest, even violent. Some cheat on their taxes or spouses; some beat their children; a few end up in barroom brawls; occasionally, one murders a rival. Nonetheless, if they are to engage in science successfully, they must exercise the scientific virtues. Early Quakerism's attributes are similar.

Attributes of early Quakerism

Like science, early Quakerism depends on experience. Experience is fundamental. Famous is Fox's "But what canst thou say?" Quakerism experiments and observes. However, while science studies external objects, Quaker experience is internal, more comparable in this respect to science's reason, an internal process, than its external objects of study.

Although early Quakerism harbors some mistrust of reason, feeling that reason may lead to "notions" rather than truth, it possesses a rational theology. Every principle in Quakerism follows logically from its belief, based on experience, that everyone has divine Light within. As Fritjof Capra notes about mystical traditions in general, experience is the ground of knowledge. Reason is for analysis and interpretation, not for acquiring knowledge.[403]

Instead, second in importance in early Quakerism is intuition. By intuition, Quakers encounter the Light in dreams, meditation, and contemplation, alone and gathered in Meetings for Worship.

Certainly, Quakerism is unworldly, its focus on the divine Light within rather than the pursuits of this world. Like science, it reaches beyond appearances to consider deeper matters. Yet, it too returns to the world to engage in practical improvements like prison reform.

Quakerism is communal. Quakers meet and work together in Meetings for Worship and Business. They also test the results of their religious experience with one another, sometimes informally, but also formally in clearness committees and through vocal messages in Meetings for Worship.

Because Quakerism respects all people equally and experience is paramount, authority vanishes. Yet, Quakers today look to the past, reading works of the founders and later writings, especially spiritual journals. Moreover, some Quakers carry more weight in Meeting than others. These are the elders, the overseers, or, in Quaker jargon, "weighty Quakers" like Fox and Barclay. Still, all remains fluid. There are neither creeds nor designated offices or leaders, yet the founders are honored and weighty Quakers heeded.

Reverence for truth is high in Quakerism. Quakers seek truth inwardly, in silence, through worship, tell the truth, and live honest lives. Yet, their truths are open to change. Truth is not fixed in creeds or catechisms, but living, experienced, revelatory. Thus, early Quakerism moved from accepting slavery to declaring it wrong later and working to abolish it. Quakerism began as a Christian sect with faith in the truth of scripture, although from the first recognizing that everyone has Light within, of whatever belief. Now, many Quakers are universalists, seeking wisdom from diverse traditions, and many are skeptical of scripture, especially if familiar with its scholarly critics. In sum, Quakers desire truth, hope they have true beliefs, but remain cautious or skeptical enough to continue searching.

Quakerism, well practiced, requires apprenticeship under the Spirit, as do all mystical traditions. Some mystical traditions add formal training under a human teacher, often lengthy. Quakerism is less formal, but no one becomes a weighty Quaker quickly, and many who have practiced for years continue to consider themselves novices. Like science, mystical religion requires habits and skills the untrained cannot use successfully. One must sit in the silence and the Light for years in order to be able to repeat the experience/experiment successfully of those already well trained.[404]

And, finally, Quakers develop certain virtues. Surely, they acquire patience, attentiveness, and humility as they await the divine voice, become imbued with the inner Light, and convey the Light's love to other people. But Quakers also emphasize truth-seeking and –telling, cooperation, and peace. These virtues, so similar to those of the scientist, are not practiced only in the Quaker community. The Quaker experience of the divine is transformative, inculcating the virtues as a way of life – at home, in school, at work, in Meeting, on vacation, and alone. Being a Quaker requires a degree of integrity, of personal integration, that being a scientist does not demand.

Overall, though, early Quakerism and science coalesce. They depend on experience, are rational and intuitive, unworldly yet concerned with the world, communal, reject authority but learn from the past, seek truth, require apprenticeship, and develop similar virtues. They form a congenial complementarity, both depending on experience, with science facing outward, Quakerism inward. They are also extreme manifestations of mind, science specializing in reason, Quakerism in intuition.[405] Indeed, Peacocke finds the spiritual and the scientific so similar, he suggests the model of bridging science and religion be replaced by that of exploring a common reality.[406]

In Quakerism's early centuries, Quakers rejected art as frivolous, merely a human creation, and turned to science to explore something superior, God's creation. Some Quakers became great scientists. Between 1851 and 1900, Quakers were forty-six times more likely to be elected to the Royal Society than were other English people.[407] Yet, it is doubtful they sought evidence for God's existence through science, for they knew science provided the wrong instrument. They did not make what philosophers term a "category mistake." Science will not discover God, nor should it.[408] The Light is within, revealed in inner experience.[409] Quakerism neither clashes with science nor depends on it for evidence of God's existence. Orthodoxy is different.

Attributes of orthodoxy

Tension arises between orthodoxy and science because orthodoxy, whether Protestant or Catholic, claims already to possess the truth, whereas science rejects authority to seek truth by its own methods and through its own experience. Orthodoxy's name itself implies possession of truth, for the Greek words from which *orthodoxy* derives mean *true opinion*. Orthodoxy's activities also demonstrate its claim to truth. The learned orthodox engage in apologetics, efforts to prove to others that the truth they possess is justified. They accuse those who disagree with them of heresy, from the Greek word for choice – "intentional decisions to depart from the right belief."[410] The orthodox develop formal statements of the truth, whether the Nicene Creed, the Augsburg Confession, or the fundamentals of Fundamentalism, then ask their members to learn them and adhere to them.

Thus, orthodoxy does not need experiment, reason, or intuition to find truth, although it may use reason to defend itself. Indeed, orthodoxy does not need to seek truth, for it has already grasped it. For orthodoxy, seeking is dangerous. It may carry the seeker away from established truth into error.

Whether orthodoxy is worldly is debatable, for it forms monastic communities based on poverty, chastity, and obedience, but also enjoys the splendors of the Vatican and the wealth accumulated through the Protestant ethic. Orthodox people may resemble the scientists who, when practicing their vocation are unworldly, but outside it may be worldly.

Orthodoxy is communal, but the community is hierarchical and depends on authority, whether Pope or scripture, creed or pastor. It looks to the past for legitimation rather than guidance. Rex Ambler notes that by Fox's time, science, with its injunction to test for oneself experimentally, began to invade other spheres of life, like politics, and Fox followed science. Religions that retained authority began to secede from the wider culture.[411]

Orthodoxy's virtues are obedience, acceptance, faith in established beliefs, and conformity. As such, orthodoxy has been and can be violent. Its urge is to force others to conform to its beliefs.

Orthodoxy and science conflict. Science threatens orthodoxy, for it may prove orthodoxy's alleged truths false and, in any case, questions authority. Orthodoxy threatens science because, if it held sway, science would cease – to search for truth when you already have it is both foolish and dangerous.

Another clash between orthodoxy and science developed with the emergence of the theory of evolution and the cosmological discovery of the big bang and the expanding universe. Orthodoxy is static, unchanging. When it developed, Christendom believed the world static and unchanging, existing just as God had created it – or as it became when rescued pairs repopulated Earth from Noah's ark after the flood. Now, science has disclosed a different world, a dynamic and evolving cosmos and biosphere, increasing in the long run in complexity, structure, and variety.[412] The dynamism of eastern religions like Taoism and Buddhism fit science's world better than the static world of Christian orthodoxy does.[413] Moreover, the eastern religions correspond to the Enlightenment's sense of liberation better than orthodoxy does,[414] despite the Biblical narrative of the Exodus and St. Paul's assurance (Gal. 4-6:10) that Jesus frees us from bondage. To hold static beliefs in a dynamic, evolving world exudes more than a whiff of contradiction.

In conclusion, orthodoxy and science conflict. Science seeks truth; orthodoxy already possesses it. Science rests on experiment and reason, orthodoxy on faith and authority and, for many, faith in authority. The scientist's virtues are honesty, humility, truth seeking and –telling, communal sharing, and peaceful dialogue; the orthodox person's virtues are obedience and faith in established beliefs. They do not dwell well together.

In contrast, science and early Quakerism complement one another. They both depend on experience. Both are rational and intuitive. Both hold similar outlooks on community and authority. They seek truth and practice similar virtues. They share an abstract methodology. They differ markedly in only three places. Science depends on external experience, Quakerism on internal. Of reason and intuition, science makes reason primary, Quakerism intuition. Scientists need only practice the scientific virtues while doing science; Quakers lead transformed and integrated lives, so they practice the virtues at all times. Even so, science and early Quaker theology reside well together, for the different emphases compose mirror images. Without contradiction, one individual can be a rational scientist and an intuitive Quaker, an experimentalist externally and internally, and consistently virtuous.

Science and early Quakerism may have similar and complementary attributes, but early Quakerism believed historical the same Christian origins narrative orthodoxy did and, for some, still does. However, the scientific saga refutes Christianity's origins narrative.

11. ORIGINS

IN THE seventeenth century, orthodoxy and Quakerism agreed the Bible relates history. God created the universe less than six thousand years ago, Adam and Eve fell, corrupting human nature, and the laws that rule the perfect heavens differ from those on our corrupted Earth. Nonetheless, science had begun its incursions. Contrary to the Bible, it discovered the Earth round, with the sun at the center of the universe. Before century's end, Newton showed the same laws rule in the heavens as on Earth. Although at times vacillating, often the orthodox response was to repress the new knowledge and persecute the scientists who discovered it. In contrast, early Quakers embraced experiment as the road to truth, and many later Quakers became scientists. Now, however, the scientific saga has scrutinized scripture, and the soul, as the seventeenth century understood it, has dissolved. This chapter explores the ramifications for Quakerism and for orthodoxy. To understand the consequences of introducing Christianity to today's scientific saga, it is necessary to begin with a brief account of the saga.[415]

The scientific saga

Today's scientific saga begins with the big bang 13.7 billion years ago. It marks the beginning of our universe. Science cannot describe the precise occasion because the known laws of physics break down before science traces events back to their beginning. However, science knows subsequent events in detail. The universe expanded and cooled, and the light elements formed, hydrogen and helium. Today, as near its beginning, the universe is about seventy-five percent hydrogen and twenty-five percent helium. The universe continued to expand and cool, as it is doing today.

Because the expanding gases were distributed somewhat unevenly, gravity began to mass the denser areas into galaxies and to coalesce the denser areas in the galaxies into stars. As the material that was to form stars grew denser, it heated, and electrons fled their atoms, exposing nuclei to each other. As nuclei randomly crashed into each other, some combined due to the laws of physics, and the heavier elements formed, eventually all those in our periodic table of the elements. Science understands in detail how the elements formed. The hydrogen and helium here today materialized shortly after the big bang; the other elements cooked in the stars. However, they did not remain caged in stars. Supernovae blew them out into interstellar space where gravity gathered them and more stars formed. In some star systems, the gases and heavier elements created planets. Our Earth is composed of many heavy elements because of its proximity to the sun, whose heat boiled surface gases away.

Earth formed some 4.6 billion years ago. At first, it was a hot and forbidding place, but eventually it cooled and stabilized sufficiently to provide a habitat for life. For a long time, only simple, unnucleated cells existed, but eventually some cell failed to digest another it had ingested, and the undigested cell provided the predator cell with a nucleus and, thus, nucleated cells evolved. Later, these formed multicellular organisms, cells specialized, sex evolved, and species proliferated. Scientists estimate from five million to a hundred million species exist today – far too many to cram into Noah's ark – and ninety-nine percent of species that once existed are extinct. Approximately a hundred thousand years ago, intelligent, self-reflective species evolved on Earth.

The universe contains many other planets. No one knows whether they, too, sustain life or evolved intelligent, self-reflective beings.[416] Moreover, no one foresees the future. Astronomers predict the sun will expand and swallow our planet four or five billion years hence. Possibly, the universe itself, as it continues to expand and cool, eventually will cease to sustain stars and provide the necessary conditions for life. However, due to lack of evidence about the future, most scientists never bother to speculate about the world's end, for it is beyond proof or disproof.[417] What is clear is that we are neither the culmination of the universe nor its reason for being, as the seventeenth century believed. We are merely a recent species on a small planet circling a typical star.

Nonetheless, the scientific saga itself has a direction. It began with energy and a soup of particles, produced the first elements, formed stars that created almost a hundred more elements, fashioned planets, spawned life, and proliferated species. As time ran, things became more complex, more diverse, and more structured, on the whole. Whether increasing complexity, diversity, and structure is the purpose of the universe is an unresolved issue, but certainly the universe does increase them. It is creative, remarkably so, and fine-tuned. It is a transformative universe. Yet, no one knows why it is here. Perhaps it simply is.

In any case, on Earth an intelligent, self-reflective species evolved. Our evolution occurred slowly, initiated by Earth's collision with an asteroid, causing a mass extinction about sixty-five million years ago, opening niches for new species to evolve. Hominoids appeared in Africa about 27 million years ago and diversified into some eighty-four species. Today, twenty-four species exist, including our own. Paleoanthropologists think ours is bipedal because climate change in Africa some 5 to 6 million years ago turned forest into savanna and made upright gait advantageous for staying cool, seeing far, and, eventually, for outlasting prey that can sprint faster than we can, but cannot maintain a protracted pace over long distances, as we can. Focusing closely on our evolution makes it clear that evolution is not designed to create us. Accidents of asteroid collision, climate change, ecological transformation, and the exigencies of evolution by natural selection combined over millions of years to produce us. Intelligent, self-reflective creatures might have evolved, instead, from the dinosaurs had not the asteroid struck. If so, the form of the species, its social arrangements, and its moral values would have differed from our own. On other planets, intelligent, self-reflective creatures may be more creative, kinder, and more spiritual than we are, or more brutal. No one knows.

Nonetheless, science finds remarkable unity in the saga. The laws of the universe are unchanging and apply everywhere. Our blood is essentially salt water. The water consists of hydrogen created in the big bang and oxygen cooked in the stars. The sodium and chlorine composing the salt emerged there, too. Our blood is the water of Earth's primordial seas, enclosed by the first cells to survive to reproduce. Moreover, all organisms possess similar DNA, indicating a common ancestor for all life on Earth. All having bilateral symmetry, as we do, possess a gene complex, the homeobox, that controls bilateral development. I have heard theologians speak of our alienation from the universe because it took 13 billion years for us to arrive, but the claim is false, influenced still by the Fall-and-exile story in Genesis 3. The universe is necessarily as old and as large as it is to provide the conditions for life to evolve and survive. Furthermore, we are connected to the big bang and the stars through the chemical elements of which we are composed. We are products of the big bang, the stars, perhaps of organic molecules scattered through the interstellar medium, and the first cells on Earth. The saga is a continuous and integrated one, resembling a novel rather than an anomalous collection of short stories or a jumble of meaningless letters. Furthermore, we are important characters in it, for through us the novel is read, if not fully understood. To incorporate today's scientific saga, seventeenth century Quaker theology needs to improve its perspective – but not much. Indeed, the scientific saga grounds it better than the Bible does.

Grounding early Quakerism

Fox, Barclay, and their contemporaries believed scripture true, that we are descended from a primordial pair who sinned and, thereby, changed human nature for the worse. Nonetheless, their central orientation to scripture treated it as a revelation of God, the Source of all, not as history or science. Moreover, they considered the narratives metaphors for spiritual relationships. Therefore, to discover its founding narratives unhistorical hardly poses a problem. In Quakerism, scripture needs only to retain its spiritual appeal.

For the type of truth it sought, Quakerism focused on experience. It accepted continuing revelation. Thus, early Quaker theology requires only a slight change of perspective to embrace science's discoveries, based on experience, as continuing revelations of God's creative work. Rather than pulling Quakerism and God apart, science increases Quakerism's understanding of divine creativity. ·

To follow the direction of the universe's development is to watch good and evil evolve inextricably together, with good maintaining the upper hand.[418] In us, our ability to cooperate produces alliances and corporations, but also massed armies that wage war. Our creativity invents art, music, literature, science, and technology, but also promulgates pornography, poisons, torture, death camps, and weapons of mass destruction. Because good and evil are inextricably intertwined, the transformation of humankind that the seventeenth century Quakers sought remains necessary, but without requiring an evil deed committed by a first couple to explain the need for transformation. Early Quakerism emphasized experience and personal and social transformation here and now rather than Jesus' crucifixion and atonement two thousand years ago. The Quakers' focus on the present and on transformation means early Quakerism hardly needs to alter its perspective to incorporate today's scientific saga of a transformative universe.

The concept of the soul might present a difficulty for a revision of early Quaker theology, but because Quakerism avoided definitions and eschewed authority, it did not tie its theology to official concepts. Barclay, for example, mentions the soul frequently,[419] but without defining it. From context, Barclay saw the soul to be that part or aspect of persons where good and evil wrestle, the facet responding to the Light favorably, where the Light within touches and transforms human nature. For orthodoxy, the soul is clearly defined as an immortal principle, created for each person, infused into the person, separable from the body, but ultimately united with it in the resurrection. By Fox's time, Rene Descartes had invented substance dualism, the body mechanical to agree with then-current science, the soul a separate substance in us (but not in other animals, who are merely mechanical beings), that which thinks and survives death. Famously, Descartes is his soul: "I think, therefore I am," he concluded. Descartes equated soul with mind.[420] The philosophical problem was how they interact, that is, how can immaterial mind/soul move mechanical body? Today, neuroscience has demonstrated the connection between mind and brain, that mind is a product of brain, so the location of the soul has shifted. Now the soul is equated with consciousness, one of the remaining inexplicable human attributes, despite multifarious efforts to explain it.[421] The soul, it seems, must remain mysterious in order to survive as a concept.

Conceptually, the soul serves two functions. It survives death, and it makes us unique among the animals. However, we do not need a separate substance to guarantee our survival of death. God merely needs to will our continued existence[422] and retain our memories. Quakerism's solution to the entire problem is simple. The Light permeates all things, including us. Unlike other animals, however, we have self-reflective consciousness and therefore can consciously communicate with the deity, the deity with us. Sit quietly, without distraction, attention turned inward, and await the Light's illumination within.

In contrast, whether Christian orthodoxy is literal or liberal, it confronts an impasse when it encounters the scientific saga.

Orthodoxy's impasse

Literal or fundamentalist orthodoxy believes the Bible true in all respects and therefore rejects the scientific saga. Its stance is comparable to the belief system of the seventeenth century except that the seventeenth century was only beginning to explore the universe, and therefore little science existed to threaten or deny. Marcus Borg separates the sort of literalism found in the seventeenth century from today's by referring to today's as "conscious literalism."[423] Today, biblical literalists knowingly battle the prevailing culture and find their beliefs ridiculed. Literalists probably believe the Thomastic concept of the soul, although it is unbiblical, a product of the Middle Ages.

In the thirteenth century, Thomas Aquinas matured the concept of the soul for orthodox Christianity. For him, God creates a spiritual substance fresh for each individual. God infuses it into the body. It is separable from the body, but not permanently separated from it, for it rejoins the body at the resurrection. Pope John Paul II reaffirmed this definition in the last quarter of the twentieth century. The definition is beyond disproof, but it fits awkwardly with modern neuroscience. Rufus Jones comments that the idea of a soul as descending from beyond, an alien substance stuck in dead matter to animate it, is an absurd idea.[424] He may be right, but it remains the view of the Catholic Church.[425]

Liberal orthodoxy is more nuanced. It accepts the scientific saga, but continues to affirm orthodox theology and orthodoxy's claim to stand on the Bible, which remains authoritative. This stance results in major difficulties.

First, if some biblical criticism is accepted, where should it cease and on what criteria? Science refutes the first several chapters of Genesis, turning the creation and flood stories into myths for liberal theology, but science also renders the empty-tomb, bodily-resurrection version of Jesus' post-crucifixion appearances unlikely and disproves the virgin birth.[426] Moreover, if no first couple sinned, then their sin did not anger God, and God needs no atonement for reconciliation with us. Yet, John Polkinghorne, physicist, Anglican priest, and acclaimed author in the field of science and religion, manages to be a thoughtful and critical scientist while swallowing Christianity whole. He offers a Trinitarian perspective on physics.[427] He relates science's meager remarks about the end of the world, finds the scientific picture futile, and so turns to the Bible, specifically the Book of Revelation, to tell us how the universe will really end.[428] Did the first-century author of Revelation know? All we can discern about him is that he experienced (or invented) some unusual visions, was a literary artist, and nearly failed to have his book accepted into the Christian canon – fragile threads with which to forecast the future of the universe, with or without the scientific saga.

Second, a world ruled by scientific laws is a difficult place for a transcendent God to act. Currently, this is a hot topic in the field of science and religion. Together, the Vatican Observatory and the Center for Theology and the Natural Sciences in Berkeley, California, devoted fifteen years and numerous conferences and publications to the topic. A major journal has recently allocated parts of two volumes to the subject.[429] Many scientifically sophisticated theologians find room for God's action in the randomness inherent in quantum mechanics or in chaotic events. However, as Nancey Murphy and George Ellis note, the consensus position for liberal theologians knowledgeable about science is that God does not intervene.[430] No transforming Light here.

Third, without the Fall, the question of our evil arises. Do we have innate tendencies to immorality? If so, why? When did evil originate? One answer receiving considerable attention now is that our tendencies toward doing harm and our sense of guilt arise in the tension between our biology and our culture.[431] However, as I discuss in the next chapter, the evidence points to a deeper origin, within our evolved nature.

And finally, Christianity places humanity at the center of a cosmic drama. God creates us, fashions Eden on Earth a home for us, we sin, and God drives us from home. Later, God sends the divine son to rescue us by dying, crucified, so God can forgive us for our sinful nature and our actual sins. In contrast, the scientific saga does not place us at the center of anything. We are late arrivals on a small planet at the edge of a galaxy in a universe that stretches 13.7 billion light years from us in all directions. Even the currently popular argument that the universe might have been designed to generate life fails before the fact that the degree of lawfulness in the universe is greater than life requires: for example, the charge on electrons is constant to more than one part in a billion, but no chemistry requires such exactitude.[432] On these four points, liberal Christian orthodoxy is in tension with the scientific saga.

Then, there is the soul. The soul provided an exciting topic early in the twentieth century, but no longer,[433] for the philosophical difficulties proved intractable. Seeing them in mid-century, Rufus Jones denies the soul is some foreign entity descended from on high. He links the soul with the self and associates the development of the self with social contact by those external to us, including God.[434]

We know several things that militate against the Thomastic or Cartesian soul. The brain is the seat of memory, consciousness, and intelligence. It contains no homunculus, a tiny figure purportedly somewhere within that guides us. Memory has no storehouse in the brain, but is scattered patterns of neural firing. And the self, although the center of conscious agency, occupies no single location, either. In contrast, specific neurons fire in practiced meditators when they meditate,[435] but this seems to prove nothing about the existence of God or the soul. The brain, it appears, has usurped the soul. Indeed, the term "soul" may be merely a metaphor for human creativity – imagination, intelligence, and freedom.[436]

All in all, accepting the scientific saga stretches liberal Christian orthodoxy to the breaking point. In a review of the literature as of 1960, John Dillenberger concludes that those Christians who accept the scientific saga reject the Christian scheme of sin and salvation and alter the traditional concept of God who becomes "the cause of everything, but the explanation of nothing."[437] In a recent review of contemporary literature, Ted Peters and Martinez Hewlett identify five problems not adequately addressed by Christians who accept the scientific saga. They are deep time, natural selection, common descent, divine action, and theodicy (why is there evil, if a good, all powerful, all knowing God created the universe?). Within these problems, they say, evolution removes purpose from the world, natural selection rests on violence and death, and God cannot act. Peters and Hewlett offer a solution: purpose resides in God and is "retrodictively imparted by God in the eschatological consummation."[438] Therefore, they join Polkinghorne in depending on eschatology to save the day, as does another celebrated author in the field of science and religion, John Haught.[439] Apparently, now that science provides a substantiated story of origins, orthodox theology can only find its own salvation in eschatology, which is airy speculation blissfully safe from scientific proof or disproof.

Some have moved from trying to reconcile orthodox Christian theology with science to rejecting theism and worshiping nature as science describes it. The movement is known as *religious naturalism*. Many of its proponents publish in *Zygon: Journal of Religion & Science*, probably because the founder was a religious naturalist, so the journal is sympathetic to their position.[440]

Science, especially evolutionary biology, sometimes tries to explain religion, but derives conflicting results.[441] And some physicists write futuristic science fiction as if it is science, seeking salvation through their peculiar brand of pseudoscience.[442]

In contrast to them all, Arthur Peacocke, biochemist and Anglican priest, calls for a radical revision of Christianity. It fails, he concludes, to fit the standards of rational inquiry. Christianity must stop clinging to authority, whether the Pope, the Bible, or the Church. To embrace authority no longer appears honest. Moreover, he says, many doctrines must go: the virgin birth, the empty tomb, original sin, and the atonement. Instead, religion and science must join hands, seeking a mutual explanation of a common reality.[443] The way to integrate science and religion is through critical realism that centers on past and present experience, continuing community, and an interpretative tradition. In religion, he notes, "The Christian mystic is your true critical realist – compelled to be aware both of the reality of God and of the utter inadequacy of human speech about him."[444]

His interest in mysticism and Christianity turns him to Jesus. Jesus, he observes, is admired outside Christianity. Jesus is a rabbi in Judaism, a prophet in Islam, a divine incarnation in Hinduism, and Buddhism appreciates his teachings, many of which resemble the Buddha's own.[445] Jesus' incarnation is not a descent from above, but a manifestation of the possibilities for all of us, he thinks, revealing what it means to be one with God. The Holy Spirit's action in us saves us now, by transforming us. The Light in John's Gospel illuminates all people, whether they know of Jesus or not.[446]

Nowhere have I seen any indication that Peacocke knows early Quaker theology, but his honesty and his knowledge of science and Christian theology led him to reinvent it. Like the early Quakers, he avoids doctrine, emphasizes experience, embraces Jesus as a universal figure rather than exclusively a Christian one, and courts mysticism. In trying to fit the religion of his ordination with the scientific saga, Peacocke arrives at early Quakerism.

Through Peacocke, who is not a Quaker, we see that early Quaker theology can incorporate the scientific saga far better than Christian orthodoxy can. Indeed, it profits from the saga, for the saga offers a more creative God than the Bible does, and its transformative world fits nicely with early Quakerism's emphasis on transformation. Early Quaker theology also benefits from a scientific perspective on human nature.

12. HUMAN NATURE

WE INTELLIGENT, self-reflective creatures emanate from the throes of evolution. We share DNA, genes, and gene complexes with other organisms. Biology classifies us with the other primates. We and the African apes spring from a common ancestor. It would be surprising, indeed, if we shared no behavioral traits or dispositions with other animals.

In the last half of the twentieth century, science developed a simple formula based on genetics that successfully models animal social behavior.[447] In words, the formula says the more closely animals are related to each other – the more replica genes they possess – the more altruistically they behave toward one another, all other things being equal. *Altruism* here is a technical, scientific term. By definition, an animal that behaves altruistically aids another animal to survive to reproduce, meanwhile foregoing some opportunity for itself to survive to reproduce. Motives are excluded. We cannot know what the animal is thinking or feeling when it behaves altruistically. Probably, not much. The science studying animal social behavior based on genetics is *sociobiology*. When applied to human behavior, it morphs into *evolutionary psychology*. This chapter asks how well early Quakerism's and orthodoxy's distinctive psychologies correspond to evolutionary psychology.

Evolutionary psychology

The theory of evolution as originally conceived built on economics, and economics in its turn rested (and still rests) on the simplifying assumption that each person is an atom, alone in the world, striving only to satisfy selfish interests. Observations of nature before Darwin, and from Darwin on, clearly refute this assumption. Many animals cooperate. They behave altruistically. Most prominent are the ants, wasps, and bees that form colonies, develop castes, and contain sterile workers, all female. Almost all come from one order of insects, the hymenoptera, also famous for its slothful male drones.

These colonial insects display peculiar genetic relationships. Almost all animals, including us, pass copies of approximately fifty percent of their genes to their offspring. This means parents and offspring are fifty percent related, siblings are fifty percent related, and subsequent relatedness declines exponentially. In the hymenoptera, however, females are seventy-five percent related and males only twenty-five percent related. The high degree of relatedness among females explains their altruism, the low degree among the males their indolence.[448] Sociobiology has now successfully predicted social behavior among thousands of species.[449]

Sociobiology applies to us and successfully predicts our behavior as well.[450] However, its range of application is limited – it hardly explains baseball, opera, or stamp collecting. Moreover, it is nondeterministic because genes alone – and certainly single genes – determine nothing. Genes work cooperatively among themselves and with their environments to produce behavior, and we, and perhaps other sophisticated animals, also use reason to direct our actions.

The foundational principle of evolution – that animals strive for resources in order to survive to reproduce – and its recent cousin, sociobiology, uncover the source of the most basic human dispositions, which I summarize simply as the four Rs. The most basic disposition, because it applies to all organisms and without it all other activities cease, is striving for resources. Every organism seeks resources or dies. The first of the four Rs is resources. We pursue them.

But for evolution to occur, acquiring sufficient resources to survive is not enough. The organism must reproduce. The second R is reproduction that, for us, means sexual reproduction. We seek sex, and most of us desire to beget children.

Reproduction generates the third R, relatives, and the altruistic behavior toward relatives sociobiology and/or evolutionary psychology explain. We treat our relatives preferentially. We give our children more love and more of our resources than we offer to other people's children. We celebrate holidays with our families, but rarely with strangers. We tend to hire relatives preferentially even though hiring them may be unfair (for others may have better qualifications) and unproductive (for our relatives may be incompetent employees). The unfair employment of relatives is *nepotism,* banned in some occupations and professions so merit and justice may prevail.

Justice is important to us. At its foundation lies the fourth and final R, reciprocity, the equal exchange of goods and services. Reciprocity underlies our commercial and justice systems. Although some other animals employ it, none makes it central as we do. Aristotle called us wise creatures *(Homo sapiens)* and Stephen Jay Gould labeled us storytellers *(Homo narrator),*[451] but they could equally well have named us the reciprocators *(Homo reciprocus).* Some sociobiologists claim reciprocity springs from genes for reciprocity rather than indirectly from our logical capacities, and I find their arguments convincing, for our distinct facility for reciprocity emerges on tests of logic. Those untrained in formal logic consistently think logically if scenarios posing logical conundrums involve reciprocity, yet their logic fails if the scenarios have a different basis.[452]

The four Rs represent our fundamental dispositions. The dispositions arise from our evolutionary heritage, and we share them with other organisms – striving for resources with all, sexual reproduction with many, altruism toward relatives with social animals, and reciprocity with other intelligent animals, almost necessarily those who can recognize and remember other individuals, recall good deeds, and assess the costs and the benefits of returning aid for aid, harm for harm.[453]

The four Rs are fundamental, but nondeterministic, especially in us. Some people starve themselves to death for a cause or follow simple, ascetic lives; others prefer a celibate existence or refrain from generating children; some abandon their relatives to venture to distant lands; others fail to reciprocate. Moreover, although foundational, the dispositions are hardly exhaustive. We display many others, usually derived from the basic four. For example, a much-studied disposition derived from reciprocity is indirect reciprocity, "the behavioral rule that says, Be nice to nice people and nasty to nasty people."[454] Derived, in turn, from indirect reciprocity are concern with reputation, displays of commitment, and moralistic manipulation and punishment. We are complex animals. We are also remarkably flexible. We can even alter our own brains by concentrating our minds![455] The 4R model is very simple. Yet, it explains much about behavior.

For example, when we include our remarkable capacity for symbolization, the four Rs explain the allure of worldliness. Perhaps the allure is obvious. Necessarily, evolution disposes organisms to seek the things of this world, for all evolved here, and creatures that failed to pursue the things of this world perished without offspring, whereas those that pursued them successfully became our ancestors. We, for example, require the resources of food, a safe place to sleep, and moderate temperatures. Therefore we hunt and gather, whether across the savannas of Africa or through the supermarkets of Chicago, construct houses, heat or air condition them, and don clothes. Then, we translate these things into symbols. We consume burgers and beer or lobster and fine wine, thereby declaring to the world our self-image and our status. Our clothes and houses reflect the same. We generate the socially acceptable number of children, then dress and educate them for success in our cultural environment. To maintain our friendships, we carefully reciprocate with commodities and social activities that also constitute appropriate symbols. Resources, relatives, and relationships become symbols of power, and if we pursue them successfully, give us real power that, in a virtuous circle, helps us pursue them successfully.

Worldliness, as such, is neither sinful nor evil. Without it, we would die individually and go extinct collectively. Yet, problems arise when we pursue the four Rs unduly. Some steal from others to enhance their resources and status. Others hire their wayward relatives and thereby destroy their own businesses. Still others pursue trophy spouses who are selfish, unloving, and philandering. Many of these pursuits end in prison or death. Yet, our nature leans toward egregious pursuit of the four Rs. We need some restraints, and cultures offer many, from religious to legal to customary. Even so, the four Rs go awry.

George Fox mentions the pursuit of resources leading public houses to encourage people to drink more than is good for them, markets replete with cheating and deceit, and the lascivious celebration of once holy days.[456] He comments on people seeking status and sex through dress so extravagant it makes them look like actors upon the stage and how they harm their domestic animals in destructive competitions and waste resources on trivialities.[457]

Even activities that appear principally religious serve the four Rs, which is why the early Quakers were wary of the worldly potential of religious ceremonies and songs. Anthropologist Brian Hayden, who worked in the Torajan highlands in Indonesia, stood aghast at the quantity of resources spent on feasts for the dead there. The highlanders slaughtered dozens or hundreds of buffalos and pigs for a single feast. In some cases, after the initial celebration, the highlanders erected a gigantic stone monument to the dead, requiring a work crew to quarry the stone, then hundreds or thousands of people from numerous villages laboring many days to move it to its place and erect it. All required food. Feeding them entailed yet more slaughter. Why such extravagance? If feted lavishly, the dead were thought to transmute into deities capable of bringing prosperity and wealth to relatives still alive.[458]

In summary, through a simplified model that captures the basic human dispositions, evolutionary psychology demonstrates that our worldliness is an attribute of our evolution. Furthermore, because we are symbol-wielding creatures, we convert our worldly pursuits into symbols, thereby sometimes destroying ourselves in their extravagant pursuit. To prosper, we need the restraints that culture can provide – although culture may, alternatively, embolden our extravagance.

In its treatment of worldliness, early Quakerism's psychological insights match those of evolutionary psychology amazingly well. In the end, each complements the other.

Early Quakerism's psychological insights

Although the early Quakers believed everyone possessed the Light within them, they distinguished between the natural person who resisted the Light and the inspired person who followed it. Because evolutionary psychology describes the natural person, the Quaker concept of the natural person is the appropriate concept of comparison.

Fox rejects the Calvinist ideas that people are so sinful they require imputed grace[459] and that the Fall transfers guilt to Adam and Eve's progeny before they themselves sin. [460] Evolutionary psychology fails to find iniquity in our origins, for we require some worldliness to survive and flourish in this life, and surely a good God wants us to survive and flourish. Indeed, the major concern of early Quakerism is not guilt or sin, per se, but worldliness, the allure of extravagantly pursuing the four Rs until one cheats one's neighbors, harms domestic animals, and wastes resources on frivolity. Fox and Barclay both view people as capable of natural affections and recognize the importance of love and social warmth in the human psyche.[461] So does evolutionary psychology, with its Rs of reproduction, relatives, and reciprocity.

Thus, for Fox and Barclay, the corruption at our Fall permits natural affection for kin and others, but also for cheating one's neighbors while appearing to reciprocate. It also allows the exercise of natural conscience and reason, and pronounces them helpful in our natural endeavors. On the other hand, Barclay clearly rejects conscience and reason as moral or spiritual guides and never claims we can know the Spirit through them. Evolutionary psychology emphasizes evolved dispositions rather than conscience or reason and, like all science, ignores spiritual matters.

In contrast, Barclay posits two natures in human beings, our natural, fallen nature and our spiritual, renewed one. He thinks they come from two seeds, one good, the other evil, and differ widely from one another – the difference between our duties to each other, as in natural affections, and our duties regarding the worship of God.[462] Brinton clarifies Barclay's comments about the good and evil seed when he avers that we have three choices upon which to center our lives: darkness, the twilight of reason, and the Light of God's presence. The darkness is not evil; however, to center our lives on it is evil.[463] His clarification is appropriate to Barclay's understanding of the Light, which does not destroy our nature as it would if our nature were evil but, instead, elevates it to supernatural life, transforming and perfecting it.[464] Two and a half centuries later, Rufus Jones agrees.[465] The idea that our nature is capable of transformation undoubtedly entails its flexibility. Although from a different stance, evolutionary psychology agrees. According to it, we have merely dispositions to behavior, flexible tendencies, and not deterministic edicts under genetic tyranny.

Therefore, as far as the natural person is concerned, evolutionary psychology and early Quakerism agree. Nothing in one contradicts the other. Indeed, augmentation by evolutionary psychology improves early Quakerism because evolutionary psychology explains the origin of our nature better than early Quakerism does, employing evidence and reason in place of mythic narratives. Evolutionary psychology also identifies our basic dispositions, explaining where worldliness springs from and how deep its roots are. Finally, it confirms the flexibility early Quakerism finds in human nature that, for example, Calvinism, economic theory, and other one-dimensional explanations deny. Indeed, it permits more natural flexibility than early Quakerism does, for it not only explains the source of natural human affection, but also permits the natural, reasoned expansion of those affections to all humanity.[466] To use a metaphor, evolutionary psychology paints the bottom of the picture and envisions the possibility of filling in the middle through reason, while allowing room at the top for spiritual transformation. Yet, it cannot posit the last, for science historically has abandoned spiritual explanations, including those for human behavior.

However, we know empirically that spiritual transformation such as the early Quakers proclaim possible for everyone happens to some. Christianity calls them saints; Buddhism, Bodhisattvas; Taoism, masters of Tao; while Hinduism says they have touched the Atman in themselves, the divine in us all. Quaker theology seems to answer what evolutionary psychology cannot, a philosophical conundrum known surreptitiously as the "problem of good." Why is there so much good in the world if we are inherently selfish? Too often, sociobiology and evolutionary psychology merely explain good away as, famously, in Richard Dawkins's *The Selfish Gene*[467] by having metaphorically selfish genes create literally selfish people. Adding Quakerism's psychology to evolutionary psychology rectifies this sorry state. Together, they explain the full range of human moral behavior, from everyday worldliness to evil to saintliness.[468] In contrast, orthodoxy possesses three psychologies, but none fits adequately with evolutionary psychology.

Orthodoxy's multiple psychologies

Three orthodox psychologies exist: Calvinism for Protestants, Thomism for Catholics, and liberalism. Therefore, the presentation here must be schematic.[469]

Calvinism maintains the Fall corrupted human beings completely. We are totally depraved. Every desire is sinful; pursuit of any R, no matter how restrained, is always sin. Neither our will nor our reason is useful. Our nature cannot be reformed; it must be replaced. Even God cannot transform us; God can only impute the grace of Christ to us so we appear righteous in the divine view while remaining actually unrighteous. Our behavior is determined, even predestined, as is our fate, whether saved or damned. In its single-minded inflexibility and sense that pursuit of the four Rs is always sinful, Calvinism contradicts evolutionary psychology at almost every point.

For Thomas Aquinas, our reason was not corrupted by the Fall. Reason can even prove the existence of God. Our psyche is tripartite and hierarchical. Ideally, and before the Fall, reason and will submit to God, the nonrational to reason, and the body to the soul. Such perfect people – Eve and Adam before the Fall – possess God's sanctifying grace. At the Fall, God withdraws sanctifying grace and the right relationship of the psychic hierarchy disintegrates. Now the soul is subject to the senses and reason to desire. Yet, choice remains. People can choose to cooperate with God, to love God and one another, as long as they have God's help. Yet, moral freedom is the freedom to do good, not the freedom to choose between good and evil.

From the perspective of evolutionary psychology – and the Bible! – a major problem with Aquinas's psychology is its ground-lessness.[470] The Bible says nothing about a tripartite psyche, and there is no reason to think one evolved. Indeed, current knowledge refutes Aquinas. Mind, or psyche, is a product of the brain. The brain has three distinct components. All vertebrates have a brain stem that regulates respiration, food, fluid, temperature, and sex. It evolved first. Next is the cerebellum. It handles inputs and outputs, but still unconsciously. It houses procedural memory that comes with practice, moving from conscious struggle to unconscious refinement, like piano playing. Overall lies the cortex where, among other things, conscious thought occurs. However, reason is helpless without appropriate emotions to guide it and constantly makes dysfunctional decisions, or fails to decide at all.[471] If, in paradise, reason once ruled emotion and the bodily functions the brain stem handles, Adam and Eve would have perished breathless, hungry, and childless, and we would not be here.

However, even if Aquinas were right, why does the hierarchy fall apart in precisely the way it does? Although detailed in its own way, Aquinas's psychology lacks particulars we find compelling. Aquinas fails to name the major and derived dispositions or to explain their origin. He fails adequately to explain our tendency toward worldliness, and certainly not our embrace of the more extravagant evils. Although it results in a richer psychology than Calvinism, Thomism fails to fit modern science in general and evolutionary psychology in particular.

Liberal theological psychology wanders through the maze of modern psychology from Carl Rogers to Carl Jung, from Sigmund Freud to John Dewey, from our inherent evil to our inherent goodness. Those who emphasize our goodness usually blame our environment or our culture for our faults and evils. However, cultures do not drop from Mars; we create them and, therefore, we must contain the seeds of their evil. A hundred fifty years ago, communism blamed the structure of society, specifically capitalism, for all human flaws. It set out to establish a different social order and create the "new person," a new human nature. History records the event. The "new person" quickly turned into the "old Adam," rapidly corrupting the new social structures. Finally the wall fell. Capitalism won because it appeals to the four Rs of human nature better than communism does. Capitalists, and most of us, seek resources for ourselves and our families plus economic reciprocity, while desiring somewhat more for ourselves than for others. Many churchgoers embrace similar values. The communists worked from a false model of human nature. Liberal theologians who joined them were similarly mistaken.

Therefore, liberal theology either clings to a false theological psychology or spreads so thinly over such a range of psychological theories that it lacks integrity. Almost the only psychological trait liberals support together is our alienation from the universe and from God. The former is false, as discussed earlier. As for the latter, some are alienated, others not, for saints dwell among us, as we know empirically. Liberal theology needs a better psychology. Maybe it should complete its embrace of the theory of evolution and turn to evolutionary psychology for its understanding of human nature. However, so far it has not done so.

In conclusion, orthodox Christian psychology fails to fit evolutionary psychology. It offers nothing positive. In contrast, the psychology of early Quakerism, in its discussion of worldliness, anticipates evolutionary psychology while suggesting how to avoid pursuing worldliness unduly. Indeed, Quakerism completes evolutionary psychology by solving the problem of good that evolutionary psychology dismisses. In response, evolutionary psychology provides support for the psychology of early Quakerism, giving it a firmer foundation and more detailed explanation than the Bible provides. As Arthur Peacocke notes, if God creates immanently, through evolution, worldly morality logically should spring from sociobiological processes.[472] The only thing needing further explanation is human saintliness, and early Quakerism's psychology explains it. Saintliness grows within us like a seed into a mature plant when we acquiesce to and cooperate with the Light within, tuning our evolved and dissonant nature into divine harmony and blessed peace.

And, so, the book draws to a close. In the final chapter, I develop a model of theology for the twenty-first century. It is firmly rooted in the theology and practice of the early Quakers, yet incorporates biblical criticism and modern science. It provides a theology for our time.

13. A THEOLOGY FOR OUR TIME

DEVELOPED religions include world-views, ethics, and practices. An intellectually viable religion will integrate these into a logical, consistent whole. An epistemically viable religion will incorporate the best current knowledge. The integration of modern science and biblical criticism with seventeenth century Quakerism provides an intellectually and epistemically functional religion. Most importantly, perhaps, is its ability to incorporate a scientific world-view.

Incorporating a scientific world-view

For philosophical reasons, science limits itself to describing the material world. However, the description of the material world it now offers from the atomic level down is nothing like matter as conceived by the early atomists or pre-twentieth century scientists. The atomists and early modern scientists thought the ultimate constituents of matter much like the material things we encounter daily, only smaller. Matter at the indivisible, atomic level was tiny, hard, round (but perhaps with hooks), particulate, inert, and, eventually, knowable. It was, in a word, lifeless. Thus, before the twentieth century, life was commonly explained by a special, nonmaterial property. Plato called it *soul* and considered the soul immortal, while Aristotle posited various types of souls for the different categories of life – vegetable souls for plants, animal souls for organisms with sensation and movement, and rational, albeit mortal souls for us. Many scientists in the early twentieth century were vitalists. They believed life required a special property beyond the constituents of matter, but ceased to call it *soul* because *soul* had religious connotations, and Christianity usually considered the soul exclusively a property of human beings, not a general life force.

However, twentieth century science altered the scientific outlook. Quantum mechanics now describes matter as both wave- and

133

particle-like, indeterminate, active, creative, and ultimately unknowable. It is, in a word, dynamic. Even virtual particle-waves exist that never quite become real wave-particles but, nonetheless, affect interactions among the particle-waves. The latest theory says underlying everything may be tiny strings whose various vibrations result in the different types of wave-particles. Strange stuff, indeed. It is so spirit-like, so ephemeral, yet sufficiently substantial when conjoined to create our universe. Is Spirit, perhaps, the ultimate, underlying reality? Are we experiencing the harmonics of Light in the vibrations of strings that produce our universe and our experiences? No one knows. We can only describe the sub-atomic level – and the spiritual realm – through metaphor.

Thus, the *Tao Te Ching* says:
There was something formless and perfect
Before the universe was born.
It is serene. Empty.
Solitary. Unchanging.
Infinite. Eternally present.
It is the mother of the universe.
For lack of a better name,
I call it the Tao.
It flows through all things.[473]

Later, the Gospel according to John 1:1-9 proclaims, "In the beginning was the Word, and the Word was with God, and the Word was God. . . . All things came into being through him. . . .The true light, which enlightens everyone, was coming into the world." Both the *Tao Te Ching* and the Bible may be referring to the same Spirit, under the imaginative distinctions of metaphor, and that same Spirit may be one with the harmonious, if metaphorical, strings of the universe. The material world science describes is remarkably spiritual.

Moreover, our universe is a transformative, creative world. The big bang produces hydrogen and helium. Gravity tugs them into galaxies and stars. The hydrogen breaks down into its constituents in the stars that fashion the heavy elements from them. Some of these elements construct a planet, Earth, where life appears and evolves into complex, structured, diverse beings using the material from the big bang and the stars plus organic matter other organisms produced. Creation and destruction contend, but creation triumphs, forming novel structures until it evolves intelligent, self-reflective creatures. These creatures, after millennia, discover how the material world came to be, then narrate the saga while, at the same time, being self-consciously spiritual creatures. Is the Spirit best described by the Hindu metaphor of Shiva Nataraja, Lord of the Dance, who is the god of death and time, but also the creative power of nature whose meditation preserves the world?

We evolved here on Earth from other primates, not only physically, but also dispositionally. We seek the four Rs. Sometimes, we chase after them. Yet, for reasons science only partly explains, we desire more than the four Rs and, in fact, feel restless and unfilled if we limit our pursuits only to them. We are creative, too, transforming old material into new. To create, we sometimes follow the four Rs, as when we transform carbonaceous deposits into refined fuels or mineral deposits into finger rings, earrings, bracelets, and necklaces. But at other times, our pursuits are more spiritual, as when Michelangelo discovered David in a block of marble or Beethoven celebrated the unity of humanity through his Ninth Symphony. Through our own transformative creativity, we enter the pattern of our creative world. We enter it, too, when we ourselves are transformed, becoming deeper, more spiritual persons, and then expressing our experiences through literature, art, dance, and song.

If, where, or when our universe will end, no one knows. However, science can predict Earth's destruction fairly accurately because it understands the formation and disintegration of stars and the mechanisms underlying them. Our sun is a typical star. It will fuse all its hydrogen and swell to a red giant star in some four to five billion years, swallowing Earth. No one knows where we will be by then. Probabilities suggest our extinction long before Earth's demise. We can no longer honestly consider ourselves the center of the universe or its sole purpose. But, then, science does not explore purposes, only materials and their interactions. Most human beings believe we have a spiritual purpose, that there is a Spirit, a Light, drawing us to itself.

The locus of the Light

Quantum mechanics and seers alike tell us that underneath the diversity we find around us, all is one. Seers find the Spirit everywhere, perceive the Light shining through all things. The renowned Chinese sage, Lao-tzu, proclaims,

The Tao can't be perceived.
Smaller than an electron,
It contains uncountable galaxies.
All things end in the Tao
As rivers flow into the sea.[474]

Such insights are few. Yet, early Quakerism, the Islamic Sufis, and many Eastern religions say the Spirit resides in us all. We can experience its presence here and now, and the experience is open to everyone.

In us, the Spirit does three fundamental things. First, it reveals itself. Many religions have sacred scriptures they claim reveal the Spirit. The early Quakers found the Light revealed in the Bible to those spiritually inspired. Later Quakers turned to science to find God in the works of the creation, God's works, that people could increasingly fathom. Because art and music are human fabrications, the early Quakers rejected them as sources of revelation. Yet, no better theologian of the Fall exists than their contemporary, the English poet John Milton, whose *Paradise Lost* deals more artfully with the subject than any other writer does. He manipulates the biblical narrative so cunningly, his rendition successfully reflects the theology of orthodox Christianity without apparently distorting the text! Music carries many people into a spiritual realm. The covenant, says Jeremiah 31:33b, is written on the human heart, so other means of teaching become redundant. Heeding early Quakers and modern biblical criticism, we find sacred scriptures transformed from authorities to companions, revealing God to us through other people's experiences and their creative recollection of them.

Second, the Spirit transforms us. Barclay relates his experience. He entered the gathering of God's people, derisively called Quakers, and felt the good in him enhanced, the evil diminished. He sought further transformation and, so, became a Quaker. Fox proclaims a new world, with a different smell and himself translated to innocence. St. Paul writes of a new creature (2 Col. 5:17). Jesus hears the voice of God at his baptism and, after a time of contemplation, returns to the Jewish homeland to begin a new mission, no longer following John the Baptist (Luke 3: 21-22; 4:1-15). He preaches the kingdom of God, among and within us, but unnoticed (Luke 17: 20-21).

Third, some transformed people carry the good news to others. The Buddha, Jesus, Mohammad, Fox, and other saints and Bodhisattvas[475] become preachers and, in literate cultures, writers. As with Tolstoy and Gandhi, they sought social transformation as well as individual liberation. They felt our freedom, and wished us to use it wisely, under the guidance of the Light. As Lao-tzu says,

> In harmony with the Tao,
> The sky is clear and spacious,
> The earth is solid and full,
> All creatures flourish together,
> Content with the way they are.[476]

The Light brings all into harmony, so carrying the good news to others is important for the flourishing of humanity on an ecologically viable Earth.

Often the early Quakers sound as if they inhabit a dualistic universe where people have two natures, the natural and the divine. However, modern science and the visions of seers render dualism unlikely. True, Quakerism's psychology is best conceived in modern terms as positing an evolved human nature resistant to the divine, and a divine nature transforming evolved human beings. Often, this is the way people experience personal transformation. The power for transformation seems a power beyond them, the breakthrough of enlightenment, whether under the Bodhi tree or on the Damascus road. However, for most people transformation occurs slowly, over a lifetime, if at all. Nonetheless, if the divine is all-pervasive, as seers state and quantum strings sing, there cannot be two natures. Dualism is impossible because all is Spirit, all is divine. Spirit pervades all nature. Matter is merely Spirit transformed. Spirit pervades us, too. We differ from the rest of nature only in being conscious of its presence. We recognize and seek the divine. Zen Buddhism says,

> The true nature of each individual person is nothing less than the Buddha nature of infinite wisdom and compassion. Only, in our normal existence we are prevented from realizing this by the operation of our minds. . . . Our task, then, is to defeat our ordinary mind so that our true nature, our Buddha nature, can take possession of us. When this happens, we attain Enlightenment.[477]

As the early Quakers knew, the Light is within everyone. We are never separated from it. However, we must cease resisting it, must approach gently in concentrated silence, to see it and learn to cooperate with it. It lies in our deepest, wordless being, beyond comprehension. Yet, living in the Light has consequences that are ethical and practical.

Ethics and practices

The great theological principle of the early Quakers is the universality of the Light. Sex does not exclude. Poverty or wealth, sickness or health, do not exclude. Behavior does not exclude. Beliefs do not exclude. Everyone, without exception, possesses the divine Light within. As the Buddhists claim, it is our true nature, but hidden from us – as we may infer from science – by the dispositions of our evolved minds.

This theology has consequences, logically entailed corollaries. If everyone has the Light within, then treating anyone violently must be rejected, for everyone warrants respect. Quakers are known for their nonviolence, not only their refusal to fight in wars, but their work to bring peace to prisons and mental health facilities, villages, cities, nations, and the world. Their God is a God of peace (2 Thess. 3:16).

Quakerism not only rejects outright violence, but also deception, manipulation, and other forms of personal abuse. If everyone has the Light within, all deserve to be told the truth. To tell the truth is, again, to treat others with respect.

With equal respect. Because everyone has the Light within, everyone is equal. As God is no respecter of persons (Rom. 2:11), so we should raise none higher than others, either. The early Quakers treated women equally with men, refused hat honor, and erased egregious titles. They also treated the American aborigines fairly. Belief in the equality of all evinces a certain humility.

A review of the four Rs shows that the simplicity of the early Quakers was more an effort to shun worldliness than to escape complexity. The early Quakers wore plain dress to avoid being distracted by the competition and expense of tracking fashions. Moreover, their hearts rested elsewhere, in the Light. Where your heart is, there your treasure will be (Matt. 6:21). They ceased to value things the evolved dispositions treat as central and, instead, sought spiritual treasures: meekness, holiness, and a peaceful, godly community with others everywhere on Earth.

If God is within, then erecting cathedrals and temples that lift gazes heavenward is incongruous, even contrary to the Spirit. God is not up there, above the azure dome of the sky, an external power to be feared and placated, but within, a humble sigh heard in inward silence without external distractions – no bells, no incense, no liturgy, no psalms, no prayers composed by a committee. Nothing, nothing at all to appeal to the evolved dispositions. And, because everyone has the Light, the Teacher within, none needs designated clergy to bring the Word to the people. People already have the Word, if only they still themselves to listen. Quietly, quietly: "The Tao never does anything, / yet through it all things are done."[478] And through it, all divine speech forms – the vocal ministry of God's word from each to all.

Under this simple but powerful theology, salvation has already come. It is available now. It consists of living in the Light, today. To worry about an afterlife is superfluous. To live in the Light is to be already saved. If so, and there is a continuing personal existence after death, entering it will be already familiar, a joy. If not, "All things end in the Tao / as rivers flow into the sea."[479] Because God is with us, we cannot break away from the divine (Rom. 8:35-39).

Here, then, is a theology that works in the contemporary world. It is a combination of the core theology of the seventeenth century Quakers whose main tenet is that everyone has the divine Light within, whether characterized as the divine Christ, the Buddha-nature, the Atman, the Tao, or simply the Islamic Sufi's love of the God who loves. It is a theology for a globalized world, crossing ethnic and religious boundaries. Yet, for the individual, it can be a theology centered not only on the divine Christ, but the historical Jesus who spoke of God within and among us, of love, of entering the kingdom of God, here and now, who practiced humility and equality and never devised a liturgy. It is, as Barclay repeatedly argues, the theology of the New Testament, while being neither doctrinaire nor exclusive.

This theology profits from modern biblical criticism. Critiques of the Bible undermine sacrificial and atonement theologies and emphasize the historical Jesus. The early Quakers minimized sacrificial and atonement theologies entirely while following the historical Jesus prior to the development of the concept. This new theology rejects sacrificial and atonement theologies while heeding the historical Jesus and finding him an exemplar fully suffused with the Light. Thus, while undermining Christian orthodoxy, modern biblical criticism supports a theology altered little from that of the early Quakers.

Modern students of ancient Christian liturgies realize we are unaware of how the early church worshiped. As Barclay notes, the Bible is replete with sayings about waiting on God, but the New Testament offers no instructions for liturgical worship. Clearly, Jesus kept his worship simple, if intense. He rejected Temple sacrifice to pray outdoors. Disturbed, he left others and prayed alone, yet gathered disciples to form communities for God. Christianity can remain Jesus- and Bible-centered, but can also welcome the metaphors and scriptures of other faiths that share the theology of the Light, practice silence to experience it, and honor the ethics of equality, honesty, simplicity, and non-violence to live in it.

Because the biblical narrative of Genesis 3 has human nature improve when Eve and Adam consume ، the fruit of the tree of knowledge, the Christian doctrine of the Fall plummets down the cliffs of scripture correctly interpreted. Science, meanwhile, destroys the narrative as history. No first couple existed, and therefore Jesus is no second Adam. Orthodox Christianity's world-view is false. To be honest, its theology must be rewritten.

Science offers a world-view to replace the fictitious orthodox Christian one. Underlying the perceptible material universe are quantum particle-waves, and perhaps quantum strings, suffusing all things, so spirit-like and active as to confound the concept of matter. Science's universe is dynamic. It has been transmuting existing material to produce increasingly complex and structured novelties for 13.7 billion years. Science reveals a transformative world. Core Quaker theology fits into this world, for it, too, is transformative. The spiritual Light pervades all. Shining in the evolved person, it transforms superficial individuals into characters of depth, purpose, and spirituality. It weakens desire for the four Rs, refocusing the person on spiritual matters far more satisfactory and fulfilling to the complex human personality than chasing the four Rs is. Sufficiently enlightened individuals may result in a transformed society, with respect for equality, truth, simplicity, and community. This theology is even an ecological theology, speaking for conserving resources by rejecting trivialities and respecting all sentient beings. This is a theology for our time.

SUMMARY OF THE ENCOUNTER WITH SCIENCE

Quakerism appears as science begins to permeate British culture, so Quakerism borrows from science – the centrality of experience, respect for intuition and reason, communal features, reformist tendencies, and an appreciation for the past without veneration of it. Science and Quakerism also have virtues in common: honesty, patience, humility, peacefulness, and unworldliness. Science and Quakerism reject orthodoxy's trust in authority and ancient truth. Thus, the increasing power of science over the following three centuries strengthens Quakerism while weakening orthodoxy.

Science discovers a changing universe that mirrors Quakerism's belief in human transformation and opposes orthodoxy's grip on stability and certainty. Science finds humanity an intimate part of the universe, challenging orthodoxy's claims of human alienation. Evolutionary psychology encounters a flexible human nature, inclined toward worldliness due to the evolution of dispositions to pursue the four Rs, but capable of either greed or generosity, lust or love, nepotism or humanism, justice for self or justice for all. Such flexibility strains orthodoxy's emphasis on sin and predestination. Quakerism, with its transformative inner Light, completes evolutionary psychology, solving the problem of good. The Light, it proclaims, leads humanity from its natural worldliness and egocentricity to acts of heroism and lives of saintliness.

Early Quakerism thinks in dualistic terms: the natural person, the divine Light. Yet, the material world science discloses at the quantum level resembles Spirit. Perhaps in the end, all is Spirit, and we differ from other animals relative to it because we become conscious of its Light and can choose to interact with it to be transformed into spiritually fulfilled beings. Such is the Quaker vision.

INFORMATION ON CONTEMPORARY QUAKERISM

THE FOLLOWING information is taken from <quaker.org>. Please consult the site for more recent information. To find an unprogrammed Quaker Meeting nearby, consult <quakerfinder.org> which locates Meetings by zip code. Information about Quaker universalism is available at <www.universalist-friends.org> (North America) and <www.qug.org.uk> (Britain).

- Ted Hoare's introductory pamphlet on the RSOF
- Hans Weening's Meeting the Spirit
- Joel Gazis-Sax's book list.
- Dan Schlitt's Bibliography of vocal ministry
- Descriptions of Religions and Ethical Systems, of the Quaker flavor
- How a Quaker Meeting for Business works.
- Quakers and the Political Process - an exhibit by Philadelphia Yearly Meeting

    The big three umbrella organizations

    - Friends General Conference – mostly unprogrammed Meetings
    - Friends United Meeting – mostly orthodox
    - Evangelical Friends International – orthodox
- Friends World Committee for Consultation
    - Africa Section
    - Section of the Americas
    - Asia/West Pacific Section
    - Europe & Middle East Section

- Quaker Retreat Centers
  - Pendle Hill – mostly unprogrammed
  - Ben Lomond Quaker Center
  - Powell House, the NYYM retreat center.
  - A retreat program of NEYM for children in grades two through six.
  - Woolman Hill, a Quaker retreat center.
  - Woodbrooke, a Quaker Study and retreat center in Birmingham, England.
  - Glenthorne Quaker Guest House and Conference Centre, Grasmere, England
  - Quaker Oaks Farm, PYM retreat center
  - Michigan Friends Center
- Friends Committee on National Legislation
- Friends Committee on Legislation of California
- Quaker Universalist Fellowship – unprogrammed
- Quaker Universalist Group (UK) – unprogrammed
- Friends for a Non-Violent World
- Friends Service Committees
  - American Friends Service Committee
  - Canadian Friends Service Committee
  - German Friends Service Committee
  - Quaker Service Australia
  - Quaker Service Norway (Kvekerhjelp)
- Friends for a Nonviolent World
- Friends for Lesbian, Gay, Bisexual, Transgender, and Queer Concerns - formerly FLGC
- Quaker House of Fayetteville NC, to aid conscientious objectors
- Peaceworkers
- Friends Council on Education The Religious Organizing Against the Death Penalty Project
- Quaker Volunteer Service and Training
- Friendly Folk Dancers
- William Penn House
- Friends Association of Higher Education
- Barclay Press
- El Salvador Project
- Friends Conference on Religion and Psychology
- Friends Bulletin

- Quaker Information Center
- New Foundation Fellowship (UK)
- New Foundation Fellowship (USA)
- Quaker Lesbian Conference
- Friends Peace Teams
- Fellowship of Quakers in the Arts
- Washington Quaker Workcamps
- Si a la Vida - a four-year old project to rescue and rehabilitate glue-sniffing street-kids in Managua, Nicaragua.
- Friends Committee on Washington State Public Policy
- Quaker Peace Centre, Cape Town, South Africa
- Quaker Experiential Service and Training, Seattle
- QUIP is Quakers Uniting In Publishing, a consortium of Quaker Publishers.
- Northern Friends Peace Board, UK
- Quaker United Nations Offices
- Quaker United Nations Office Geneva
- Quaker United Nations Office New York
- Quaker Council for European Affairs
- The James Nayler Foundation for the treatment of violent behaviour and severe personality disorder
- Clarence and Lilly Pickett Fund for Quaker Leadership
- The Tract Association of Friends
- Friends House Moscow
- Beacon Hill Friends House
- Friends International Library - Publishing in Russia and Chechnya
- The Leaveners, Quaker Performing Arts Project.
- Friends Christian Ministries, Conservative Friends in Greece.
- The Dallas Peace Center
- Quaker Social Witness Committee of the Central & Southern Africa Yearly Meeting
- QUEST: Quaker Ecumenical Seminars in Theology
- Costumed Ministry
- Right Sharing of World Resources
- Evangelical Friends Mission
- The Coalition for Hispanic Ministries
- Quakerdale, a family service organization in IA.
- Women's Goals 2000
- Fellowship of Friends of African Descent

- Friends Fiduciary Corporation
- Friends Committee on Scouting
- Friends Services for the Aging
- Quaker Theological Discussion Group
- Friends Center of Ohio Yearly Meeting
- Quaker Conflict Resolution Network (forming)
- Quaker G.O.P., Guerilla Outreach Project
- North Carolina Friends Historical Society
- School of the Spirit Ministry
- The Friendly Gangstaz Committee
- Quaker Bolivia Link
- Friends Afghan Concern
- Project Lakota
- World Gathering of Young Friends, Lancaster University, August 2005
- Nontheist Friends
- White's Residential and Family Services, Inc., a Quaker child care agency of Indiana Yearly Meeting.
- Latvian Quaker Group
- Arlington Friends House, a cooperative near Boston
- ProNica supplies funds, equipment and information to established community organizations in Nicaragua.

Friends and Nature

- Friends Energy Project
- Quaker Earthcare Witness
- PYM Committee in Unity with Nature

Writings

- Autobiography of George Fox
- Journal of John Woolman
- Another Journal of John Woolman
- George Keith. New-England's spirit of persecution. [New York], 1693.
- Travels in Virginia and North Carolina. George Fox. 1672.
- Lucretia Mott
- William Penn – America's First Great Champion for Liberty and Peace
- Pirates of Penn's-ance

- The Richmond Declaration
- Alice Stokes Paul
- Rev Thomas Beals, first Friends minister in Ohio
- Susan B. Anthony
- Thomas S. Clarkson, Abolitionist, author of *A Portraiture of Quakerism.*
- Wordsworth and the Problem of Action: The White Doe of Rylstone – also contains a reference to the above Thomas Clarkson's book *A Portraiture of Quakerism.*
- Larry Kuenning's collection of historical Quaker e-Texts
- The Quaker Writings Home Page, Peter Sippel, editor.
- Margaret Fell's essay "Women's Speaking Justified, Proved, and Allowed of by the Scriptures, All such as speak by the Spirit and Power of the Lord Jesus. And how Women were the first that Preached the Tidings of the Resurrection of Jesus, and were sent by Christ's own Command, before he Ascended to the Father, John 20. 17" (written about 1666 or 1667).
- The Memoirs of Sunderland P. Gardner
- U of Mich Quaker Collection
- Herstory – interesting little stub of a page
- Quakers and the Arts Historical Sourcebook
- The Record of a Quaker Conscience: Cyrus Pringle's Diary – A Vermont Quaker in the Civil War.
- Voltaire and the Quakers – about, not by.
- The New Foundation Fellowship (UK), proclaiming the Christian Quaker message.
- James Nayler's Spiritual Writings
- Chuck Fager's Bit of Quaker Bible Study
- One Quaker's approach to the Bible
- Glenside Friends Meeting's paper on disownment
- The Declaration of Life – an anti-death-penalty request
- Chuck Fager's position paper against the Richmond Declaration.
- Peter Sippel's "Quaker Bible Study of Jonah"
- Hans Weening's Meeting the Spirit: An introduction to Quaker beliefs and practices
- Bibliography for Christology and the historical Jesus
- Davide Melodia's Il Signore del Silenzio / The Lord of Silence
- Chuck Fager's missive on why liberal Quakers are authentic Quakers.

- Movies on Peace and War Issues Recommended by Quakers
- "Without Apology" – Larry Ingle reviews Chuck Fager's new Book
- Thou and You – an article by Alan Firth on the demise of thee/thou in the English language
- NYYM Renewal Report
- A list of Quaker periodicals
- Quaker Electronic Archive
- Jim Flory's Contemplative Quakerism page
- Tom Cunliffe's Journey of Life
- Advertising blurb for R. Charles Stevens's Letters from Viet Nam - the author's experience in Viet Nam during 1962-4 serving as concientious objector.
- Quaker Science Fiction
- Merle Harton publishes *The New Quaker*
- Herb Lape wrote a case study describing how NYYM has dealt with minutes on sexuality.
- Eden Grace has a paper explaining Quaker decision-making practice and its theological presuppositions.
- Bill Samuel maintains a Quaker Information site.
- Lord, make me an instrument of your peace.
- Geraldine Glodek's Friends and Fragrances
- The AFSC's seminal pamphlet, Speak Truth to Power
- Quaker humor, some in Danish.
- The Quaker Economist – economics with a Quaker twist.
- Quaker and Ecumenical Essays by Eden Grace
- A Gay Quaker Timeline, 1820s-1950s
- Thoughtful, compassionate, and generous: American Heroes of the Asian Prodigal
- Confronting the Powers that Be: A Study Guide by Vern Rossman
- A World of Love and How to Get There
- A Short History of Conservative Friends
- Quaker Pamphlets
    - William Penn Lectures
    - Pendle Hill Pamphlets
    - Quaker Universalist Pamphlets
- Letters from Viet Nam, a book by Charles Stevens.
- A Statement from Leaders of Friends Organizations in the U.S.

- A Quaker in the Military – Reflections of a Pacifist among the Warriors
- Quakers in the News – a blog format summary of news that mentions Quakers

Young Friends

- Phila. Young Adult Friends
- Philadelphia Yearly Meeting Young Friends
- NYYM Powell House Young Friends
- Young Friends General Meeting, Britain
- Northwest Yearly Meeting Young Adult Friends
- Baltimore YM Young Adult Friends
- Young Adult Friends Email Contacts Worldwide
- Baltimore Yearly Meeting Young Friends
- Australian Young Friends
- Quaker Service Opportunities
- NC Yearly Meeting Young Friends
- FCNL's Young Adult Friends
- YouthQuake

Performing and Visual Artists and Musicians

- John McCutcheon, Hammer Dulcimer Musician
- Aaron Fowler: Interactive programs (having nothing to do with compute for teachers, parents and students.
- Aaron Fowler & Laura Dungan
- Carrie Newcomer, Folk Musician
- Piano Classic Restorations...by Terry Farrell, offering complete rebuilding of fine grand pianos.
- Bill Harley, singer/storyteller.
- Women's History ALIVE! One woman plays by Sandra Hansen
- Sara & Kamila (Singer-Songwriters)
- Bonnie Raitt, singer, songwriter, activist.
- Mercedes Walker - documentary filmmaker, singer, musician & activist
- Kat Burke - singer, songwriter, performer.
- Melanie Weidner - artist.
- Arthur Davenport has a CD out.
- Joyce Rouse, aka EarthMama.
- Spontaneous Combustion Storytellers - Tom & Sandy Farley
- Dan Gilliam

- Arthur Fink Photography
- Adrian Martinez

Summer Camps

- Camp Katahdin - run by Douglas W. Crate Sr.
- Friends Camp, a Quaker summer camp for youth.
- Friends Music Camp at Olney Friends School in Barnesville, OH
- Camp Onas
- Camp Woodbrooke
- Farm & Wilderness
- Catoctin, Shiloh and Opequon, all run by Baltimore Yearly Meeting and therefore unprogrammed.
- Camp Quaker Haven, Kansas.
- Ben Lomond Quaker Center, a week-long preteen camp.
- Sierra Friends Camp, in the Sierra Nevada foothills of California.

APPENDIX TWO

ON METAPHOR

EARLY QUAKERISM is replete with metaphors. A modern understanding of metaphor helps fit early Quakerism into our milieu. For this purpose, the definition of metaphor can be simple. It is something that stands for something else, whether by relationship, resemblance, association, or convention. It resembles symbol and suggests analogy. In the past, linguists usually limited metaphors to language and treated them as decorations on otherwise direct, literal prose. However, in recent years specialists have studied metaphor and language through neurobiology and bodily experience. These studies are revolutionizing the classical understanding of metaphor, reversing former beliefs. Under the new conception, metaphor is primary, while apparently direct, literal language derives from metaphors. Metaphors, in their turn, arise from bodily experience that, in its turn, springs from brain states. Thus, a transformation has occurred in understanding how language develops and metaphor functions. Knowing a little about this transformation will facilitate comprehension of the metaphor of the Light within as well as the early Quaker use of metaphor in general.

Language and metaphor

We know now, as we did not know in past centuries, that thoughts, emotions, self-concepts, language, and brains are intimately connected. Without brains, the others fail to appear. Brains are material, functioning through known laws of physics and chemistry. They develop partly through the activity of our genes and their products and partly through experience. Genes and their products provide a rough draft of the brain, and then experience revises the draft to create our individual, working brains by adding or deleting neurons and strengthening or weakening connections among them. A famous slogan in neurobiology is, "Neurons that fire together wire together." The stronger the wiring is among neurons that once fired together, the more likely the neurons will fire together again. Thus, neurons develop group interactions.

We also know certain brain states result in consciousness, although no one knows exactly how. However, it seems clear now that our consciousness indirectly informs us about our brain states. We do not know our brain states, as such, for we cannot view our brains, and even if we could, scanning our neuronal activity would not tell us what we feel or perceive. Rather, our neurons speak to us in metaphors. They say to us, "This brain state feels like pain, while this one looks like red, yet this other sounds like a C sharp," so we know our brain states through conscious, experiential metaphors for them. This is the primary, fundamental sense in which language is metaphoric. It is about brain states typically produced by experience of the outer world. Communication between conscious beings tells them about each other's brain states, too, metaphorically, as long as the connections and communications are reliable.[480]

When we float in the womb and later emerge as infants without language, our bodily experiences wire the brain in certain ways. Then, when language develops, we build on these bodily experiences to speak of intangible things like social relationships, mental states, and abstractions. Language about social relationships, mental states, and abstractions is always metaphorical, founded on bodily experiences, whereas language about bodily experiences is more immediate. We may discuss space and bodily experiences without drawing on social relationships, mental states, or abstractions, but we cannot discuss social relationships, mental states, or abstractions without employing metaphors derived from bodily experiences. [481]

Our basic metaphors are bodily: up-down, front-back, light-dark, male-female,[482] force (push-pull), container (in-out), journey (along a path to a destination), and seeing as knowing.[483] The journey metaphor may well be the source of our grammar, giving us subjects (the one who moves), verbs (the movement), and objects (the thing moved or moved toward),[484] so that grammar springs from experience rather than being lodged somehow in our genes.

An example of the up-down metaphor may show how metaphors develop out of bodily experiences. Up is generally turned into a metaphor for happiness, more, control, virtue, and health; down into one for sad, less, uncontrolled, bad, and ill. We know this because we say things like "I'm really up for that!" and "I'm too down today to do anything but weep." The stock market goes up and down. Things are good when it goes up, bad when it goes down. A bad person puts me down; a good one fixes things up. People come down with the flu. We express all these states in terms of the metaphors of up-down derived from physical states. Why is up good and down bad? Because of our natural, bodily states. When we are sad, our posture droops, we lie down and become unconscious and vulnerable in sleep, we sit or lie down when ill, are knocked down when defeated, and fall down dead. In contrast, when we are well and happy, we walk erect. The victor who has knocked us down comes out, literally, on top.[485]

Moreover, our experience is organized. It is not a blooming, buzzing confusion, but comes in small stories we combine to make larger ones.[486] We do not vision water as splashing from nowhere, but as pouring from a cup. The cup did not fill itself magically; someone filled it. Now we combine these two small stories to make a larger one about how a certain amount of water got from A to B. We also develop metaphors from our stories.[487] We know a literal, physical story about the liberation of the Jews from oppression in Egypt, and so we make a metaphor of it to apply to our own liberation from an obsession, an unhappy marriage, or a miserable job.

That we form language and metaphor from experience means our thought develops because we are embodied. To think is to be a body with the experiences of sensing, manipulating objects, and moving across landscapes. When we think, as when we dream, our thoughts detach from muscular activity, but we base the metaphors used on previous muscular activity that wired our brains to connect the directions up with happy and down with sad.[488]

For diurnal creatures such as ourselves, who move about and actively accomplish undertakings during daylight, but sleep unconscious and vulnerable in the dark, light provides a basic metaphor. It connotes goodness. It aligns with another basic metaphor, seeing as knowing. We speak of acquiring knowledge as enlightenment and even name the century following Newton, when we thought we could know nature completely and that reason could lead us individually and collectively, the Enlightenment. For us, dark is dangerous and bad. Light stands for goodness, safety, help, and rescue.

All these are metaphors because, literally, light consists of photons. Photons strike the eye, cause neurons to fire, and create an experience of brightness. Because light is such a powerful metaphor for us, and one that connotes safety and goodness, we use it to speak of God. "God is light and in him there is no darkness at all," says 1 John 1:5. John is not thinking of photons. He is presenting a God who is good, safe, and a help in time of trouble. The early Quakers used the metaphor of light for God so frequently, they became known as "Children of the Light."[489] We always approach God through metaphor, whether philosophically or experientially.[490]

God as metaphor

The abstract, philosophical concepts of God are metaphors in the primary sense. The concepts depend on basic bodily metaphors formulated to suggest God's attributes are infinite. The bodily metaphor of force becomes omnipotence; that of seeing as knowing turns into omniscience; and up is good converts to omnibenevolence and transcendence. Because falling is dangerous, we speak positively of being grounded. Paul Tillich famously calls God the "ground of all being." We see one thing affect another, talk of causes, try to imagine an infinite regress, fail, and conjecture a first cause, God. These metaphors for God spring from our bodily experiences, but not from our experience of God. Fox disparagingly calls them "notions."

In contrast, Fox, Barclay, and many other early Quakers speak of direct, unmediated experiences of God, and some describe their experiences in journals, sermons, and letters. These descriptions, too, are metaphoric, but in a second sense. Now, metaphors stand for inner experiences neither mediated immediately through bodily experience nor learned abstractly from others. They resemble the experiences we have in dreams, but are far more orderly.

Fox's journal contains many examples of this second kind of metaphor. Early on, when he is in despair over his spiritual condition, but finds other people, especially clergy, unhelpful, he reports,

> And when all my hopes in them [clergy] and in all men were gone, so that I had nothing outwardly to help me, nor could

tell what to do, then, Oh then, I heard a voice which said, 'There
is one, even Christ Jesus, that can speak to thy condition', and
when I heard it my heart did leap for joy. Then the Lord did
let me see why there was none upon the earth that could speak
to my condition, namely, that I might give him all the glory.[491]

Fox hears a voice, but not an outward one. We could not today
capture the voice he heard on a tape recorder. Afterward, he has a
realization, seeing his previous condition in a new light. (It is impossible to avoid the basic metaphors such as seeing as knowing!) Fox
builds his metaphor on the bodily experience of hearing external,
human voices. Evidently, he is not deliberately making a metaphor,
as he often does, but reporting what he hears inwardly, which seems
like a voice speaking words. He also builds the metaphor on cultural experience, for he lives in a Christian country with height-
ened religious awareness because embroiled in a civil war over
Christianity. In a Buddhist culture, the voice might well have told
him that Buddha could speak to his condition or in a Hindu culture, Krishna or Shiva. The joy accompanying his inner experience
is typical of mystical experiences.

Fox might protest that the voice he hears is not a metaphor, but
a voice. However, he does not literally hear sound any more than
he literally sees why no one could help him. He does not see anything. He has a realization. Likewise, the voice he hears is an inner
one. It involves neither sound waves nor ears. He expresses his experience in metaphors, mediated indirectly by previous bodily experiences.

In the *Apology*, Barclay recounts his own initial religious experiences:

> For when I came into the silent assemblies of God's people, I
> felt a secret power among them, which touched my heart. And
> as I gave way to it, I found the evil in me weakening, and the
> good lifted up. . . . And I hungered more and more for the
> increase of this power and life until I could feel myself perfectly
> redeemed. [492]

The basic metaphor for him is force (power) that moved him
emotionally (touched my heart), on the analogy of forces moving
material objects. Good, of course, is up. Barclay's hunger, too, is
metaphoric, based on bodily experience. He cannot eat this power.
And, finally, he interprets his experience in terms familiar in his

culture, as one of redemption. Barclay is sophisticated about such experiences. He mentions that, "Since the Spirit of God is within us, and not merely outside us, it speaks to our spiritual ear, and not to the physical one."[493]

In his study of spiritual experience among the early Christians, James Dunn says St. Paul characterizes God as a Spirit that works at the center of human beings, an inner power that transforms persons in the direction of love and liberation.[494] For Paul as for Fox and Barclay, the spiritual experience is of an inner power that changes people, liberating them, leading them toward goodness.

Mystics in the East – Hindu, Buddhist, and Taoist – speak of a power that creates unity and/or is unity itself. They experience the universe as one and the self becoming one with it.[495] Although mystics from the western traditions are cautious about saying they and God are one (to say so was heresy, and dangerous), they also write about the unity of all things and/or oneness within multiplicity.[496] It is perhaps foolish to speculate, but possibly such experiences draw on bodily experience in the womb or an infant's feeling of melding with the mother while nursing. In any case, the experience usually arises after years of effort to eliminate all empirical awareness from consciousness. The result might have been simply to render the practitioner unconsciousness, but seems, instead, to culminate in a sense of naked self merging with a larger Self, the Self or Soul of the universe.[497]

Quakers typically do not strive for such high mysticism but, instead, seek unity with God so they may enact the divine will in the world. Yet, they too write of a Spirit of unity, one that draws all who earnestly seek the Spirit into a unified community. Thus, they are aware of the human community God creates and of unity with God, if not normally of the unity of all things in God.

People who have (or think they have) direct, unmediated experiences of God all speak of the ineffability of their experiences, and all who try to express those experiences wrestle with the difficulties of language and logic. They say they must use metaphors, albeit inadequate metaphors, because a direct, literal description is impossible.[498] When they try to be direct and literal, they only speak of what God is not. We now know that here, too, they must depend on metaphor.

Thus, the term *God* often refers to a notion, a philosophically and rationally derived concept, based metaphorically on bodily experience, but not on direct experience of the divine. To talk of unmediated experiences of God also requires metaphor. Now we know why. Language is fundamentally metaphoric. The early Quakers chose well when they used Light as their most frequent metaphor for God. Light is fundamental for diurnal creatures and brings with it connotations of knowing, goodness, safety, and help. The Quakers' Light within has no photons, but is a metaphor for their interior, personal experience of God, a God they may experience as brightness, and certainly know as good, who leads to righteousness all who seek transformation.

The Quakers' Light is not literal. Yet, many experience the Light as radiance. Undoubtedly, it enlightens them. Fox writes of seeing "an ocean of darkness and death, but an infinite ocean of light and love, which flowed over the ocean of darkness. And in that also I saw the infinite love of God."[499] So metaphoric is Fox's Light that he actually writes more than thirty times of hearing it![500] Of course, he does not derive the metaphor solely from experience. Fox memorized the Bible; many Quakers knew it well. One of their favorite passages comes from the opening verses of John's Gospel:

In the beginning was the Word, and the Word was with God, and the Word was God. He was in the beginning with God. All things came into being through him, and without him not one thing came into being. What has come into being in him was life, and the life was the light of all people. The light shines in the darkness, and the darkness did not overcome it. . . . [It is] the true light, which enlightens everyone. . . . And the Word became flesh [in Jesus] and lived among us. (John 1:2-9, 14)

This passage as well as others from the New Testament suggested to the early Quakers that the Light is God, but also Jesus the man, the risen Christ, the Holy Spirit, and the Spirit that gives life. The early Quakers were not Trinitarians, and to try to read them as if they were leads only to confusion. As a scholar of early Quakerism notes, God, Father, Christ, Holy Spirit, Light, Truth, Power, all Quaker terms, stand for a single reality, and the Quakers regard Jesus as filled with this reality, which they also call the eternal Christ.[501]

Indeed, *Light* seems a better term than *God* to represent Quaker perception, just because God is the more abstract, philosophical concept, often a rational construct, whereas Light stands for an inner experience of radiance and enlightenment believed to be divine. Moreover, Light is not specific to a single religious culture, as the terms Holy Spirit, Christ, Jesus, covenant, cross, bread, and lamb are. The early Quakers think anyone can experience this Light, whether Christian or not, yet they are perfectly aware that Muslims, for example, will not refer to it as Christ, although Muslims may well think the historical Jesus imbued with it.

So the second sort of metaphor is for inner, mystical experience believed to be of divine origin, perhaps best captured by the Quaker metaphor of the Light within. However, the early Quakers use metaphor in a third way. They turn doctrines and biblical and historical characters and narratives into metaphors for the inner experience of the divine Light. Thus, they stack metaphors on metaphors.

Metaphor in original Quakerism

Fox knows his Bible thoroughly, and he draws on its doctrines, characters, and narratives to develop metaphors for the inner life. The astute commentator, Douglas Gwyn, observes that Fox "interpreted the entire Bible through a powerful, typological hermeneutic that made a wide range of biblical symbols, motifs and history into living realities in the human consciousness."[502] A few examples from Fox's writings may clarify Gwyn's insight.

In a sermon delivered in Barbados, Fox calls the Sabbath a figure (meaning a sign of what is to come, a metaphor) for our rest in Christ. He explains that a Sabbath rest for Christians means stopping one's egocentric works at any time to wait quietly on God so we may do works centered in God rather than in ourselves.[503] Fox is thus reading the establishment of a day of rest in Jewish law as foreshadowing Christian respite in Christ – a respite from selfishness. He turns the Sabbath into a metaphor for an inner, spiritual state.

In the same sermon, he refers to the gospel as "the power and wisdom of God."[504] Usually, we think of the gospel either as the narratives about Jesus in the Gospels or the good news of Jesus as savior. In contrast, Fox equates the gospel with the Light within, which is the power and wisdom of God. He transforms the devil in a similar manner, the devil who, in the New Testament and seventeenth century England, is an evil spirit, a bad character, a demon. Fox transforms this demon into a power, "[The Seed] destroys the devil which is the power of death."[505]

In a paper dated 1654, Fox refers to Jesus as the "substance" and the Jewish Temple and its rites as "shadows and types" of Jesus. These are seventeenth century terms, now mostly outdated. In modern English, Fox is saying that Jesus is the real thing, the Temple a mere shadow that prefigures Jesus' advent. Once the real thing has arrived, the shadow is no longer necessary and can be eliminated. The Temple and its rites were outward, says Fox, then adds that baptism, Eucharist, and psalm singing are also outward.[506] Fox equates Christian rites and rituals with the Jews' rites and rituals whose dispensation he believes has ended. True Christianity, Fox thinks, is inward, the meeting between people and the Light; Christian rituals, like those of the Jews, are mere shadows, no longer required because Christ, the real thing, is here, within all people.

Fox even treats the virgin birth as a metaphor. He writes of "that which calls your minds out of the earth, turns them towards God, where the pure babe is born in the virgin mind."[507] The mind is to turn from the earthly to the spiritual, become empty, be infused with divinity, and birth the divine. He also converts the plantations in America into metaphors, admonishing those going to the new world to "Keep your own plantations in your hearts, with the spirit and power of God."[508] The practice of interpreting outward events and biblical narratives as metaphors for the spiritual life does not cease with Fox. As late as 1830, Elias Hicks refers to Jesus' cross as the law of God written on the heart, the Light within.[509]

Barclay emphasizes metaphor as much as Fox does, and he uses the word. He comments on the story of the woman at the well in Samaria. In it, he notes, Jesus turns the water drawn by the Samaritan woman into a metaphor for eternal life. Then Barclay adds, "Christ's statement about his blood was also a metaphor."[510] Barclay has been arguing against the Catholic doctrine of transubstantiation in which the bread and wine literally become Christ's body and blood. Barclay says, no, Jesus is speaking metaphorically of the inner, spiritual feeding on Christ, not literal drinking.

In the same way, Barclay comments that St. Paul's "one loaf" of which "we all partake" does not refer to outward bread, but to "inward spiritual bread," the Spirit of Christ.[511] Barclay, like Fox, also equates God's judgment, which both think occurs now within people, with Jesus' death. God's judges people here and now, and crucifies their sins here and now, before God raises them to new life, spiritually, here and now.[512] True religion is for Barclay, as for Fox, inward, and salvation occurs in this life.

Like Fox, Barclay sometimes seems remarkably modern. Barclay's cosmology is seventeenth century cosmology, and he probably fuses the biblical and Copernican worlds much as Milton does. For him, as for Milton, heaven is a place above the clouds. Yet, Barclay comments that the Quakers' opponents' "notion of God as being beyond the clouds will be of little use to them if they also cannot find him near them."[513] In today's cosmology, heaven cannot be a place above the clouds, for Earth and the solar system are part of the starry heavens. We necessarily must find God near us, if we are to locate the divine at all. To find God near, of course, is to seek the Light within, not as an imaginative metaphor based on photons or a philosophical speculation built on bodily experience, but as a divine power permeating all nature, including our own, to enlighten and transform those willing to mature spiritually. For Quakers, the Light is a transforming inner power, and they develop a theology for it.

REFERENCES

Akenson, Donald Harman. 1998. *Surpassing Wonder: The Invention of the Bible and the Talmuds*. New York: Harcourt Brace & Company.

Alcock, John. 2001. *The Triumph of Sociobiology*. Oxford: Oxford University Press.

Alper, Matthew. 2001. *The "God" Part of the Brain: A Scientific Interpretation of Human Spirituality and God*. Boulder, Colorado: Rogue Press.

Ambler, Rex (ed.). 2001. *Truth of the Heart: An Anthology of George Fox 1624-1691*. London. Quaker Books.

Aune, David E. 1983. *Prophecy in Early Christianity and the Ancient Mediterranean World*. Grand Rapids, Michigan: William B. Eerdmans.

Barclay, Robert. See Freiday.

Barclay, Robert. 1676. *The Anarchy of the Ranters and Other Libertines*. Kessinger Publishing's Rare Mystical Reprints.

Benson, Lewis. 1966, 1973. *Catholic Quakerism: A Vision for All Men*. Philadelphia: Philadelphia Yearly Meeting.

Borg, Marcus and Ray Riegert (eds.). 1997. *Jesus and Buddha: The Parallel Sayings*. Berkeley, California: Seastone.

Borg, Marcus J. 1994. *Jesus in Contemporary Scholarship*. Valley Forge, Pennsylvania: Trinity.

Borg, Marcus J. 2003. *The Heart of Christianity: Rediscovering a Life of Faith*. San Francisco: HarperSanFrancisco.

Boulding, Kenneth E. 1964. *The Evolutionary Potential of Quakerism*. Wallingford, Pennsylvania: Pendle Hill (Pamphlet 136).

160

Boyer, Pascal. 2001. *Religion Explained: The Evolutionary Origins of Religions Thought.* New York: Basic Books.

Brinton, Howard H. 1957. *Quakerism and Other Religions.* Wallingford, Pennsylvania: Pendle Hill (Pamphlet 93).

Brinton, Howard H. 1973. *The Religious Philosophy of Quakerism: The Beliefs of Fox, Barclay, and Penn as Based on the Gospel of John.* Wallingford, Pennsylvania: Pendle Hill.

Brinton, Howard H. 2002. *Friends for 350 Years: The History and Beliefs of the Society of Friends since George Fox Started the Quaker Movement* (updated by Margaret Hope Bacon). Wallingford, Pennsylvania: Pendle Hill Publications.

Brown, Warren S. 1998. "Cognitive Contributions to the Soul" in Brown et al., 99-125.

Bullinger, Ethelbert W. 1975. *A Critical Lexicon and Concordance to the English and Greek New Testament.* Grand Rapids, Michigan: Zondervan.

Burdick, Winifred. 1986. "Sources of Universalism in Quaker Thought" in *The Quaker Universalist Reader Number 1: A Collection of Essays, Addresses and Lectures.* Landenberg, Pennsylvania: Quaker Universalist Fellowship, pp. 49-67.

Burke, T. Patrick. 1996. *The Major Religions: An Introduction with Texts.* Cambridge, Mass.: Blackwell.

Buss, David M. 1999. *Evolutionary Psychology: The New Science of the Mind.* Boston: Allyn and Bacon.

Cadbury, Henry Joel [1953] 1996. *A Quaker Approach to the Bible.* Landenberg, Pennsylvania: Quaker Universalist Fellowship.

Calvin, John [1559] 1995. *Institutes of the Christian Religion* (tr. Henry Beveridge). Grand Rapids, Michigan: Wm. B. Eerdmans.

Capra, Fritjof. 2000. *The Tao of Physics: An Exploration of the Parallels between Modern Physics and Eastern Mysticism* (4th Edition, updated). Boston: Shambhala.

Catechism of the Catholic Church. 1994. Mahwah, New Jersey: Paulist Press.

Chaisson, Eric J. 2001. *Cosmic Evolution: The Rise of Complexity in Nature.* Cambridge, Mass: Harvard University Press.

Chilton, Bruce. 1994. "The Eucharist – Exploring its Origins." *Bible Review*, **10**, #6 (December), pp. 40-41.

Clifford, Anne M. 1998. "Biological Evolution and the Human Soul: A Theological Proposal for Generationism" in Peters 1998, 162-73.

Cooper, Wilmer A. 1990. *A Living Faith: An Historical Study of Quaker Beliefs.* Richmond, Indiana: Friends United Press.

Cross, F. L. and E. A. Livingstone (eds.) *The Oxford Dictionary of the Christian Church.* Oxford: Oxford University Press.

Crossan, John Dominic. 1991. *The Historical Jesus: The Life of a Mediterranean Peasant.* San Francisco: HarperSanFrancisco.

Damasio, Antonio R. 1994. *Descartes' Error: Emotion, Reason, and the Human Brain.* New York: G. P. Putnam's Sons.

Damasio, Antonio. 1999. *The Feeling of What Happens: Body and Emotion in the Making of Consciousness.* New York: Harcourt Brace and Company.

Dandelion, Pink (ed.). *The Creation of Quaker Theory: Insider Perspectives.* Burlington, Vermont: Ashgate.

Darwin, Charles [1871] 1981. *The Descent of Man, and Selection in Relation to Sex.* Princeton, New Jersey: Princeton University Press.

Davies, Paul. 1998. "Is the Universe Absurd?" in Peters, Ted. *Science and Theology: The New Consonance.* Boulder Colorado: Westview, 65-76.

Davies, Paul. 1999. *The Fifth Miracle: The Search for the Origin and Meaning of Life.* New York: Simon and Schuster.

Dawkins, Richard. 1976. *The Selfish Gene.* New York: Oxford University Press.

Dennett, Daniel C. 1991. *Consciousness Explained.* Boston: Little, Brown and Company.

Dillenberger, John. 1960. *Protestant Thought and Natural Science: A Historical Interpretation.* Notre Dame, Indiana: University of Notre Dame Press.

Douglas, J. D. (ed.) 1990. *The New Greek-English Interlinear New Testament* (tr. Robert K. Brown and Philip W. Comfort). Wheaton, Illinois: Tyndale House.

Dunn, James D. G. 1970. *Baptism in the Holy Spirit.* London: SCM. Johnson.

Dunn, James D. G. 1975. *Jesus and the Spirit: A Study of the Religious and Charismatic Experience of Jesus and the First Christians as Reflected in the New Testament.* London: SCM Press Ltd.

Dyson, Freeman J. 2002. "Science & Religion: No Ends in Sight" in *The New York Review of Books* 49 (March 28), 4-6.

Eddington, Arthur Stanley. 1929. *Science and the Unseen World.* London: George Allen & Unwin Ltd., 45.

Edelman, Gerald M. 2004. *Wider than the Sky: The Phenomenal Gift of Consciousness.* New Haven: Yale University Press.

Edelman, Gerald M. and Guilio Tononi. 2000. *A Universe of Consciousness: How Matter Becomes Imagination.* New York: Basic Books.

Ehrman, Bart D. 1993. *The Orthodox Corruption of Scripture: The Effect of Early Christological Controversies on the Text of the New Testament.* New York: Oxford University Press.

Ehrman, Bart D. 2003. *Lost Christianities: The Battles for Scripture and the Faiths We Never Knew.* Oxford: Oxford University Press.

Feinberg, Todd E. 2001. *Altered Egos: How the Brain Creates the Self.* Oxford: Oxford University Press.

Finkelstein, Israel and Neil Asher Silberman. 2001. *The Bible Unearthed: Archaeology's New Vision of Ancient Israel and the Origin of Its Sacred Texts.* New York: Free Press.

Fox, George [1694] 1997. *The Journal of George Fox* (ed. John L. Nickalls). Philadelphia. Religious Society of Friends.

Fox, George [1831] 1990. *The Works of George Fox, Vol. IV. The Doctrinals, Vol. I.* State College, Pennsylvania: New Foundation Publications.

Fox, George, [1831] 1990. *The Works of George Fox, Vol. III. The Great Mystery.* State College, Pennsylvania: New Foundation Publications.

Freiday, Dean (ed.) 1967. *Barclay's Apology in Modern English.* Newberg, Oregon. Barclay Press.

Freiday, Dean and Arthur O. Roberts (eds.) 2001. *A Catechism and Confession of Faith by Robert Barclay*. Newberg, Oregon. Barclay Press.

Friedman, Richard Elliott. 1987. *Who Wrote the Bible?* New York: Harper & Row.

Funk, Robert W., Roy W. Hoover, and the Jesus Seminar. 1993. *The Five Gospels: The Search for the Authentic Words of Jesus.* San Francisco: HarperSanFrancisco.

Gorman, George H. 1973. *The Amazing Fact of Quaker Worship.* London: Quaker Home Service.

Gould, Stephen Jay. 1999. *Rock of Ages: Science and Religion in the Fullness of Life.* New York: Ballantine Publishing Group.

Greene, Brian. 1999. *The Elegant Universe: Superstrings, Hidden Dimensions, and the Quest for the Ultimate Theory.* New York: W. W. Norton & Company.

Greenfield, Susan. 2000. *The Private Life of the Brain: Emotions, Consciousness, and the Secret of the Self.* New York: John Wiley & Sons.

Gribbin, John and Mary. 2000. *Stardust: Supernovae and Life – The Cosmic Connection.* New Haven: Yale University Press.

Gwyn, Douglas. 1986. *Apocalypse of the Word: The Life and Message of George Fox (1624-1691).* Richmond, Indiana: Friends United Press.

Gwyn, Douglas. 2004. "Apocalypse Now and Then: Reading Early Friends in the Belly of the Beast" in Dandelion, Pink (ed.). *The Creation of Quaker Theory: Insider Perspectives.* Burlington, Vermont: Ashgate, pp. 132-3.

Hamm, Thomas D. 2004. "'New Light on Old Ways': Gurneyites, Wilburites, and the Early Friends" in *George Fox's Legacy: Friends for 350 Years, Quaker History* **93**, #1 (Spring). Haverford, Pennsylvania: Friends Historical Association.

Haught, John F. 2000. *God after Darwin: A Theology of Evolution.* Boulder, Colorado: Westview.

Hayden, Brian. 2003. *Shamans, Sorcerers, and Saints: A Prehistory of Religion.* Washington: Smithsonian Books.

Hedrick, Charles W. 2002. "The Thirty-four Gospels: Diversity and Division Among the Earliest Christians. *Bible Review* **18** (3), 20-31,46-47.

Hefner, Philip. 1993. *The Human Factor: Evolution, Culture, and Religion*. Minneapolis, Fortress.

Henderson, Stephen. 2004. "Let there be Lasers: The Illumination of Charles Townes" in "Historic Milestones," Radnor, Pennsylvania: John Templeton Foundation, June.

Hick, John. 1986. "Christ in a Universe of Faith" in *The Quaker Universalist Reader Number 1: A Collection of Essays, Addresses and Lectures*. Landenberg, Pennsylvania: Quaker Universalist Fellowship, pp. 27- 35.

Hicks, Elias. [1832] 1969. *Journal of the Life and Religious Labors of Elias Hisks*. New York: Arno Press and the New York Times.

Hinshaw, Cecil E. 1964. *An Apology for Perfection*. Wallingford, Pennsylvania: Pendle Hill (Pamphlet 138).

Irons, William. 2004. "An Evolutionary Critique of the Created Co-Creator Concept" in *Zygon* **39** (December), 773-90.

Johnson, Luke Timothy. 1998. *Religious Experience in Earliest Christianity: A Missing Dimension in New Testament Studies*. Minneapolis: Fortress.

Jones, Rufus M. 1904/23. *Social Law in the Spiritual World: Studies in Human and Divine Interrelationship*. New York: Swarthmore.

Jones, Rufus M. 1936. *The Testimony of the Soul*. New York: Macmillan.

Jones, Rufus M. 1941. *Spirit in Man*. Stanford, California: Stanford University Press.

Jones, Rufus M. undated. *Rethinking Quaker Principles*. Wallingford, Pennsylvania: Pendle Hill (Pamphlet 8).

Kelly, Thomas R. 1941. *A Testament of Devotion*. San Francisco: HarperSanFrancisco.

Knowles, Elizabeth (ed.). 2004. *Oxford Dictionary of Quotations*. Oxford: Oxford University Press.

Lacey, Paul A. 2003. ". . . *The Authority of Our Meeting Is the Power of God.*" Wallingford Pennsylvania: Pendle Hill (Pamphlet 365).

Lakoff, George and Mark Johnson. 1980. *Metaphors We Live By.* Chicago: University of Chicago Press.

Lakoff, George and Mark Johnson. 1999. *Philosophy in the Flesh: The Embodied Mind and Its Challenge to Western Thought.* New York. Basic Books.

Lewin, Roger. 1998. *Principles of Human Evolution: A Core Textbook.* Oxford: Blackwell.

Llinas, Rodolfo R. 2001. *I of the Vortex: From Neurons to Self.* Cambridge, Mass.: MIT Press.

McGinn, Colin. 1999. *The Mysterious Flame: Conscious Minds in a Material World.* New York: Basic Books.

Meier, John P. 1994. *A Marginal Jew: Rethinking the Historical Jesus. Vol. II. Mentor, Message, and Miracles.* New York: Doubleday.

Midgley, Mary. 1992. *Science as Salvation: A Modern Myth and Its Meaning.* London: Routledge.

Mitchell, Stephen (tr. and ed.). 1988. *Tao Te Ching.* New York: HarperPerennial.

Morse, Melvin with Paul Berry. 1990. *Closer to the Light: Learning from the Near-Death Experiences of Children.* New York: Ivy Books.

Murphy, Nancey and George F. R. Ellis. 1996. *On the Moral Nature of the Universe: Theology, Cosmology, and Ethics.* Minneapolis: Fortress.

Murphy, Nancey. 1998. "Human Nature: Historical, Scientific and Religious Issues" in Brown, Warren S., Nancey Murphy, and H. Newton Malony (eds.). *Whatever Happened to the Soul? Scientific and Theological Portraits of Human Nature.* Minneapolis: Fortress, 1-29.

Newberg, Andrew, Eugene D'Aquili, and Vince Rause. 2001. *Why God Won't Go Away: Brain Science and the Biology of Belief.* New York: Random House.

Ornstein, Robert. 1993. *The Roots of the Self: Unraveling the Mystery of Who We Are.* San Francisco: HarperSanFrancisco.

Peacocke, Arthur. 1984. *Intimations of Reality: Critical Realism in Science and Religion.* Notre Dame, Indiana: University of Notre Dame Press.

Peacocke, Arthur. 1993. *Theology for a Scientific Age: Being and Becoming – Natural, Divine, and Human* (Enlarged Edition). Minneapolis: Fortress.

Peacocke, Arthur. 2000. "Science and the Future of Theology: Critical Issues" in *Zygon: Journal of Religion & Science* 35, 119-140.

Peacocke, Arthur. 2001. *Paths from Science toward God: The End of All Our Exploring*. Oxford: Oneworld.

Pelikan, Jaroslav. 1971. *The Christian Tradition: A History of the Development of Doctrine, Vol. 1. The Emergence of the Catholic Tradition (100-600)*. Chicago: University of Chicago Press.

Penington, Isaac. 1998. *The Light Within and Selected Writings of Isaac Penington*. Philadelphia: The Tract Association of Friends.

Peters, Ted and Martinez Hewlett. 2003. *Evolution from Creation to New Creation: Conflict, Conversation, and Convergence*. Nashville: Abingdon Press.

Pius XII [1950] 1956. *Human Generis. The Papal Encyclicals in Their Historical Context*. (ed. Ann Fremantle, tr. Ronald A. Knox). New York: New American Library.

Polkinghorne, John. 2002. *The God of Hope and the End of the World*. New Haven: Yale University Press.

Polkinghorne, John. 2003. "Physics and Metaphysics in a Trinitarian Perspective" in *Theology and Science* 1 (April), 33-49.

Punshon, John. 1987. *Encounter with Silence: Reflections from the Quaker Tradition*. Richmond, Indiana: Friends United Press.

Pym, Jim. 2000. *The Pure Principle: Quakers and other Faiths*. York, England: William Sessions Limited.

Rachels, James. 1991. *Created from Animals: The Moral Implications of Darwinism*. New York: Oxford University Press.

Ridley, Matt. 1996. *The Origins of Virtue: Human Instincts and the Evolution of Cooperation*. New York: Penguin.

Roberts, Arthur O. 2004. "'Come in at the Door!' How Foxian Metaphors of Salvation Speak to Evangelical Friends." *Quaker Hisotry*, **93**, 1 (Spring). *George Fox's Legacy: Friends for 350 Years*. Friends Historical Association, pp.112-115.

Schwabe, Calvin W. 1999. *Quakerism and Science*. Wallingford, Pennsylvania: Pendle Hill (Pamphlet 343).

Schwartz, Jeffrey M. and Sharon Begley. 2002. *The Mind and the Brain: Neuroplasticity and the Power of Mental Force*. New York: ReganBooks.

Shackle, Emma. 1978. *Christian Mysticism*. Butler, Wisconsin: Clergy Book Service.

Sharman, Cecil W. (ed.). 1980. *No More but My Love: Letters of George Fox 1624-1691*. London: Quaker Home Service.

Sharman, Cecil W. 1991. *George Fox and the Quakers*. London: Quaker Home Service.

Sheeran, Michael J. 1996. *Beyond Majority Rule: Voteless Decisions in the Religious Society of Friends*. Philadelphia: Philadelphia Yearly Meeting of the Religious Society of Friends.

Siegel, Daniel J. 1999. *The Developing Mind: Toward a Neurobiology of Interpersonal Experience*. New York: Guilford.

Singer, Peter. 1981. *The Expanding Circle: Ethics and Sociobiology*. New York: Farrar, Straus & Giroux.

Skinner, Max and Gardiner Stillwell. 2001. *That Thy Candles May Always Be Burning: Nine Pastoral Sermons of George Fox*. Camp Hill, Pennsylvania: New Foundation Publications, 224, in a sermon of Fox dated London, 1681, 24th Day, 3rd Month.

Smolin, Lee. 1997. *The Life of the Cosmos*. New York: Oxford University Press.

Spencer, Carole D. 2004. "Holiness: The Quaker Way of Perfection" in Dandelion, pp. 149-71.

Stace, W. T. 1960. *Mysticism and Philosophy*. Los Angeles: Jeremy P. Tarcher, Inc.

Steere, Douglas V. 1984. *Quaker Spirituality: Selected Writings*. Mahwah, New Jersey: Paulist Press.

Stephen, Caroline Emelia. [1890] 1995. *Quaker Strongholds*. Chula Vista, California: Wind and Rock Press.

Taber, William and Frances. 1994. *Building the Life of the Meeting*. Melbourne Beach, Florida: Southeastern Yearly Meeting of the Religious Society of Friends.

Turner, Mark. 1996. *The Literary Mind.* New York: Oxford University Press.

Underhill, Evelyn. [1911] 1990. *Mysticism: The Preeminent Study in the Nature and Development of Spiritual Consciousness.* New York: Doubleday.

Wilber, Ken. 1998. *The Marriage of Sense and Soul: Integrating Science and Religion.* New York: Broadway Books.

Wildman, Wesley J. 2004. "The Divine Action Project, 1988-2003" in *Theology and Science* 2 (April), 31-75.

Williams, Patricia A. (forthcoming). "How Evil Entered the World: An Exploration through Deep Time" in Hewlett, Martinez and Ted Peters (eds.). *The Evolution of Evil.* Vandenhoeck and Ruprecht.

Williams, Patricia A. (forthcoming). *Revealing God: A New Theology from Science and Jesus.*

Williams, Patricia A. 2001a. *Doing without Adam and Eve: Sociobiology and Original Sin,* Fortress Press, 2001.

Williams, Patricia A. 2001b. *Where Christianity Went Wrong, When, and What You Can Do About It.* Philadelphia: Xlibris.

Williams, Patricia A. 2003. "Jesus as a Friend." *Friends Journal* 49 (December), pp. 11-13, 35.

Wills, Garry. 2004. "What Is a Just War?" *New York Review of Books,* 51, 18 (November 18), pp. 32-35.

Wilson, David Sloan. 2002. *Darwin's Cathedral: Evolution, Religion, and the Nature of Society.* Chicago: University of Chicago Press.

Wilson, Edward O. 1975. *Sociobiology: The New Synthesis.* Cambridge, Mass.: Belknap.

Woolman, John. 1984. "Abridgment of the Journal of John Woolman" in Douglas V. Steere. *Quaker Spirituality: Selected Writings.* Mahwah, New Jersey: Paulist Press, pp. 161-237.

ENDNOTES

1. I would like to thank all who have commented on drafts of part or the whole of the manuscript: Chris Collins, Lynette Friesen, Barbara Hershkowitz, Paul Laughlin, Charles Tolbert, Bruce Wollenberg, and Jay Worrall.
2. Freiday, Dean (ed.) 1967. *Barclay's Apology in Modern English*. Newberg, Oregon. Barclay Press. I refer throughout to this text.
3. Freiday, Dean and Arthur O. Roberts (eds.) 2001. *A Catechism and Confession of Faith by Robert Barclay*. Newberg, Oregon. Barclay Press.
4. Barclay, Robert. 1676. *The Anarchy of the Ranters and Other Libertines*. Kessinger Publishing's Rare Mystical Reprints.
5. Fox, George [1694] 1997. *The Journal of George Fox* (ed. John L. Nickalls). Philadelphia. Religious Society of Friends, 39.
6. Aune, David E. 1983. *Prophecy in Early Christianity and the Ancient Mediterranean World*. Grand Rapids, Michigan: William B. Eerdmans, 203.
7. Sharman, Cecil W. 1991. *George Fox and the Quakers*. London: Quaker Home Service, 67.
8. Aune, 191.
9. Benson, Lewis. 1966, 1973. *Catholic Quakerism: A Vision for All Men*. Philadelphia: Philadelphia Yearly Meeting.
10. Punshon, John. 1987. *Encounter with Silence: Reflections from the Quaker Tradition*. Richmond, Indiana: Friends United Press.
11. Hicks, Elias. [1832] 1969. *Journal of the Life and Religious Labors of Elias Hicks*. New York: Arno Press and the New York Times, 355.
12. Borg, Marcus J. 2003. *The Heart of Christianity: Rediscovering a Life of Faith*. San Francisco: HarperSanFrancisco, 188.
13. Kelly, Thomas R. 1941. *A Testament of Devotion*. San Francisco: HarperSanFrancisco, 97.
14. Fox 1997, 27.
15. Fox 1997, 11.
16. Johnson, Luke Timothy. 1998. *Religious Experience in Earliest Christianity: A Missing Dimension in New Testament Studies*. Minneapolis: Fortress, 182-3.

17. Dunn, James D. G. 1970. *Baptism in the Holy Spirit.* London: SCM. Dunn, 1975. Johnson.
18. Brinton, Howard H. 2002. *Friends for 350 Years: The History and Beliefs of the Society of Friends since George Fox Started the Quaker Movement* (updated by Margaret Hope Bacon). Wallingford, Pennsylvania: Pendle Hill Publications, 19.
19. Brinton 2002, 13-17.
20. Boulding, Kenneth E. 1964. *The Evolutionary Potential of Quakerism.* Wallingford, Pennsylvania: Pendle Hill (Pamphlet 136), 13.
21. Gwyn, 65. Fox in a sermon dated London, 21st day, 3rd month 1678, quoted in Skinner and Stillwell, 177;
22. Freiday, 90.
23. Part III says more about our evolution and its consequences for human nature.
24. Freiday, 103-4.
25. Freiday, 42.
26. Freiday, 91.
27. Freiday, 91.
28. Brinton 2002, 44.
29. Freiday, 92.
30. Freiday, 92.
31. Darwin, Charles [1871] 1981. *The Descent of Man, and Selection in Relation to Sex.* Princeton, New Jersey: Princeton University Press, 71-72.
32. Brinton 2002, 44.
33. Brinton 2002, 248.
34. Jones, Rufus M. undated. *Rethinking Quaker Principles.* Wallingford, Pennsylvania: Pendle Hill (Pamphlet 8), 30.
35. Roberts, Arthur O. 2004. "'Come in at the Door!' How Foxian Metaphors of Salvation Speak to Evangelical Friends." *Quaker Hisotry*, 93 #1 (Spring). *George Fox's Legacy: Friends for 350 Years.* Friends Historical Association, pp.112-115.
36. Gwyn, Douglas. 1986. *Apocalypse of the Word: The Life and Message of George Fox (1624-1691).* Richmond, Indiana: Friends United Press, 83.
37. Skinner, Max, and Gardiner Stillwell. 2001. *That Thy Candles May always Be Burning: Nine Pastoral Sermons of George Fox.* Camp Hill, Pennsylvania: New Foundation Publications, 224, in a sermon of Fox dated London, 1681, 24th Day, 3rd Month.
38. Discussed at length in Part II.
39. Freiday, 85.
40. Freiday, 39.
41. Freiday, 24-25.

42. Hinshaw, Cecil E. 1964. *An Apology for Perfection*. Wallingford, Pennsylvania: Pendle Hill (Pamphlet 138), 14-15.
43. Freiday, 85.
44. Freiday, 85.
45. More on this in Part II.
46. Freiday, 103.
47. Hinshaw, 11.
48. Johnson, 60
49. The paragraph is condensed from Johnson 60-65.
50. In a sermon dated London, 24th day, 3rd month, 1681, quoted in Skinner and Stillwell, 228.
51. In a sermon dated London, 9th day, 4th month, 1674, quoted in Skinner and Stillwell, 68.
52. Freiday, 17.
53. Freiday, 16. Original in italics.
54. Freiday, 28.
55. Freiday, 44-45.
56. Fox 1990, Vol. IV, 154; 1997, 17
57. Freiday, 27.
58. The early Quakers read the King James translation of the Bible. Dean Freiday uses various translations in his updated version in Barclay's works. I use the New Revised Standard Version throughout, even when quoting the Bible from Freiday. I also distinguish half-verses, so the first half of John 6:5 would be 6:5a, the second half 6:5b.
59. Freiday, 330-31.
60. Johnson, 4.
61. Dunn 1975, 202.
62. Freiday, 31.
63. Fox 1997, 17.
64. In a sermon dated London, 25th or 30th day, 3rd month, 1675, quoted in Skinner and Stillwell, 113.
65. Ambler, 186.
66. In Ambler, 30-38.
67. Brinton, Howard H. 1973. *The Religious Philosophy of Quakerism: The Beliefs of Fox, Barclay, and Penn as Based on the Gospel of John*. Wallingford, Pennsylvania: Pendle Hill, 27.
68. Punshon, 13.
69. Freiday, 3.
70. In Ambler, 72.
71. Fox 1997, xxvi.
72. Fox 1997, 33.
73. Freiday, 21-22.
74. Freiday, 25.

75. Freiday, 33.
76. Freiday, 43-44.
77. All information about near death experiences is from Morse, Melvin with Paul Berry. 1990. *Closer to the Light: Learning from the Near-Death Experiences of Children.* New York: Ivy Books, 131-144.
78. Johnson, 181.
79. Freiday, 87.
80. Jones, undated, 31.
81. Kelly, 19.
82. Fox 1997, 27.
83. Fox 1997, 200.
84. Freiday, 13.
85. Freiday, 389.
86. Part III discusses this at length.
87. Shackle, Emma. 1978. *Christian Mysticism.* Butler, Wisconsin: Clergy Book Service, 36.
88. Kelly, 9-10.
89. Johnson, 6-9.
90. Freiday, 411.
91. Freiday 162-3.
92. Fox 1977, 20, 27, and 30 respectively.
93. Freiday, 93 and 166, respectively.
94. Freiday 166; Fox 1997, 33.
95. Brinton, Howard H. 1957. *Quakerism and Other Religions.* Wallingford, Pennsylvania: Pendle Hill (Pamphlet 93), 6.
96. Shackle, thesis of book.
97. Brinton 2002, 73.
98. Gorman, George H. 1973. *The Amazing Fact of Quaker Worship.* London: Quaker Home Service, 7.
99. Freiday, 259.
100. In Ambler, 62-4.
101. Freiday, 280.
102. Penington, Isaac. 1998. *The Light Within and Selected Writings of Isaac Penington.* Philadelphia: The Tract Association of Friends, 25. Language changes over time. Not only have styles of punctuation and spelling fluxuated since the seventeenth century, but words have changed meaning. Therefore, works quoted come from versions with updated language. Moreover, paraphrases are loose, even for the updated versions, which could be updated further. For example, the Muslims known to seventeenth century Britains were Turks, so when they say "Turk" they mean what we mean by "Muslim." When Penington writes of coals heaped together warming each other, I add that, separated, they grow cold. The addition occurs because we are less familiar with coals than were people in the

seventeenth century who heated and cooked with wood. When Barclay uses "self-will," I use "egocentricity," a nonexistent word in Barclay's time, but with clear meaning in ours.

103. Brinton 2002, 215, and 108 respectively.
104. Brinton 2002, 73-75.
105. Freiday, 264.
106. Punshon, 90. The reference is to Genesis 1:27.
107 . In Ambler, 24.
108. In Ambler, 86.
109. Freiday, 240.
110. Freiday, 255.
111. Freiday, 248, 264-5.
112. Freiday, 252.
113. Freiday, 298-9.
114. Pym, Jim. 2000. *The Pure Principle: Quakers and other Faiths*. York, England: William Sessions Limited, 48-53.
115. Brinton 2002, 88-90.
116. This is the thesis of Ambler's comments on Fox in Ambler's anthology, v-xiv and 150-201.
117. In Ambler, 34-6.
118. In Ambler, 60.
119. Freiday, 263-4.
120. Freiday, 259-261.
121. Gwyn 1986, 169-70.
122. Spencer, Carole D. 2004. "Holiness: The Quaker Way of Perfection" in Dandelion, 158.
123. Freiday, 277-9.
124. Brinton, 77-80.
125. Dunn, 222.
126. In Ambler, 68-70.
127. In Ambler, 14, 72.
128. Freiday, 218.
129. Freiday, 218.
130. Brinton 2002, 219.
131. Stephen, Caroline Emelia. [1890] 1995. *Quaker Strongholds*. Chula Vista, California: Wind and Rock Press, 93-6.
132. Fox 1997, 189.
133. Stephen, 34-5.
134. Britain 2002, 109.
135. Britain 2002, 117.
136. Dunn, 263.
137. Dunn, 264.
138. Dunn, 283.
139. Freiday, 258.

140. Freiday, 200.
141. Freiday, 202.
142. Freiday, 200.
143. Freiday, 171.
144. Freiday, 180-3.
145. Freiday, 220.
146. Freiday, 228-9.
147. Fox 1997, 184-9.
148. Stephen, 65.
149. A few Protestant denominations consider the water, bread, and wine merely symbolic, but in both the Eastern Church and most of the Western Church, they transmit God's grace, however that is defined exactly.
150. Freiday, 303.
151. Information for the terms is from Bullinger, Ethelbert W. 1975. *A Critical Lexicon and Concordance to the English and Greek New Testament.* Grand Rapids, Michigan: Zondervan, 515.
152. Pelikan, Jaroslav. 1971. *The Christian Tradition: A History of the Development of Doctrine, Vol. 1. The Emergence of the Catholic Tradition (100-600).* Chicago. University of Chicago Press, 162-163.
153. Freiday, 312-13.
154. Freiday, 177.
155. Freiday, 243.
156. Freiday, 301. The quotation is in italics in the original.
157. Freiday, 311.
158. Freiday, 313.
159. Freiday, 263.
160. Meier, John P. 1994. *A Marginal Jew: Rethinking the Historical Jesus. Vol. II. Mentor, Message, and Miracles.* New York: Doubleday, 40 and 55.
161. Pelikan, 166.
162. Funk, Robert W., Roy W. Hoover, and the Jesus Seminar. 1993. *The Five Gospels: The Search for the Authentic Words of Jesus.* San Francisco: HarperSanFrancisco, 270.
163. Freiday, 337-8.
164. Freiday, 339.
165. Freiday, 339.
166. Freiday, 337.
167. Freiday, 340.
168. Freiday, 345.
169. Freiday, 327-333.
170. Freiday, 360.
171. Cooper, 92.
172. Funk, Hoover, and the Jesus Seminar, 388.

173. Crossan, John Dominic. 1991. *The Historical Jesus: The Life of a Mediterranean Peasant.* San Francisco: HarperSanFrancisco, 360-5.
174. Pelican, 166.
175. Chilton, Bruce. 1994. "The Eucharist – Exploring its Origins." *Bible Review,* **10,** #6 (December), pp. 40-41.
176. Williams, Patricia A. 2001b. *Where Christianity Went Wrong, When, and What You Can Do About It.* Philadelphia: Xlibris, 111-15.
177. Fox 1997, 345.
178. Sheeran, Michael J. 1996. *Beyond Majority Rule: Voteless Decisions in the Religious Society of Friends.* Philadelphia: Philadelphia Yearly Meeting of the Religious Society of Friends, 6.
179. Sheeran, vii.
180. Sheeran, 32.
181. Barclay, 66.
182. Barclay, 5-6, 66, 77. The Catholic Church declared the Pope infallible only in 1870. In the seventeenth century, Catholics rested much authority on church councils. The counter-Reformation Council of Trent (1545-63) was especially powerful and decisive for the Catholic Church.
183. Barclay, 78-9.
184. Barclay, 79.
185. Barclay, 81-2.
186. Stephen, 132.
187. Fox 1997, 418-19.
188. Fox 1997, 445. The reference is to Colossians 1:23: "...the gospel that you heard, which has been proclaimed to every creature under heaven."
189. Dunn, 183-8.
190. Dunn, 299-300. The quotation is on 300 and is in italics in the original.
191. Dunn, 359-60.
192. Ambler, 159.
193. Taber, William and Frances. 1994. *Building the Life of the Meeting.* Melbourne Beach, Florida: Southeastern Yearly Meeting of the Religious Society of Friends, 17.
194. Fox 1997, 24. He refers to a "mixed multitude" because he is speaking to a group composed of diverse, and sometimes warring, Protestant sects.
195. Fox 1997, 109. The sermon was at Firbank Fell in 1652 before about a thousand people. A plaque now marks the rock ledge from which Fox spoke.
196. Barclay, 9-10.
197. Ambler, 188-9.

198. Penington, 33-36.
199. Lacey, Paul A. 2003. ". . . *The Authority of Our Meeting Is the Power of God.*" Wallingford Pennsylvania: Pendle Hill (Pamphlet 365), 32-3.
200. Barclay, 29.
201. Sheeran, 34.
202. Barclay, 7.
203. Gwyn 1986, 198.
204. Sheeran, 221-3.
205. Fox 1997, 373.
206. Brinton 2002, 131.
207. Sheeran, 100.
208. Sheeran, 104.
209. Lacey, 32.
210. Brinton, 141.
211. Almost everything in this paragraph is from Sheeran, 53-61.
212. Brinton, 133.
213. Brinton, 139-141.
214. Sheeran, 81-84.
215. Paragraph condensed from Sheeran, 66-69.
216. Sheeran, thesis of book.
217. The paragraph is a condensation of Stephen, 135-144.
218. Fox 1997, 170.
219. Stephen, 133.
220. Sheeran, 24-28.
221. Fox 1997, 445.
222. Freiday, 50.
223. Freiday, 51-55.
224. Ambler, 187.
225. Fox, 33.
226. The Pope is only believed infallible when speaking *ex cathedra* on faith and morals. The Catholic Church does not claim him infallible in other situations or on other subjects.
227. Brinton 2002, 227-228.
228. Brinton 2002, 232.
229. Cooper, 101.
230. Lacey, 6.
231. Fox 1997, 263.
232. Freiday, 397.
233. Freiday, 389.
234. Freiday, 394.
235. Freiday, 390.
236. Fox 1997, 280.
237. Fox 1997, 406-7.

238. Freiday, 385-6.
239. Freiday, 363.
240. Freiday, 362.
241. Freiday, 362. Original in italics.
242. Stephen, 103.
243. Freiday, 366.
244. Freiday, 372.
245. Freiday, 375.
246. Freiday, 392-3. Quotation on 392.
247. Fox 1997, 36.
248. Fox 1997, 666-668; in Skinner and Stillwell, 24-30, 85-6.
249. Freiday, 403.
250. In Skinner and Stillwell, 15-19.
251. Fox 1997, 157.
252. Fox 1997, 150.
253. Fox 1997, 169-170.
254. Freiday, 415-6.
255. Freiday, 412.
256. Freiday, 415.
257. Freiday, 531.
258. Freiday, 391-5.
259. Gwyn 1986, 41.
260. Stephen, 110-13.
261. Freiday, 405-6. Quotation, 406.
262. Freiday, 408-10.
263. Freiday, 436. He seems not to reject serious drama. The Restoration of 1660 saw the opening of the theaters in England, which were closed under the Commonwealth. The late 1600s is the era of the comedy of manners. Some are competent literature, but none is weighty.
264. Freiday, 394.
265. Fox 1997, 37.
266. Fox 1997, 205-6. The first quotations are on 205, the last on 206.
267. Woolman, John. 1984. "Abridgment of the Journal of John Woolman" in Douglas V. Steere. *Quaker Spirituality: Selected Writings*. Mahwah, New Jersey: Paulist Press, 176-7.
268. Woolman, 183-4. Quotation, 184.
269. Woolman, 215.
270. Cooper, 109.
271. Freiday, 411-430.
272. Fox 1997, 65.
273. Fox 1997, 197.
274. Fox 1997, 380.
275. Fox 1997, 389.

276. Fox 1997, 349.
277. Fox 1997, 399-402.
278. Freiday, 429-430.
279. Brinton 2002, 199.
280. Wills, Garry. 2004. "What Is a Just War?" *New York Review of Books*, 51, 18 (November 18), p. 32.
281. Freiday, 430 and 434. Quotation, 434.
282. Brinton 2002, 184-194.
283. Brinton 2002, 270-71.
284. I cover this information, and more, plus some details of biblical scholarship in *Doing without Adam and Eve: Sociobiology and Original Sin*, Fortress Press, 2001. My *Where Christianity Went Wrong* offers an introduction to New Testament scholarship. Both contain extensive references. A popular, fascinating book on the Hebrew Scriptures by a renowned biblical scholar is Friedman, Richard Elliott. 1987. *Who Wrote the Bible?* New York: Harper & Row. For a scholarly approach, see Finkelstein, Israel and Neil Asher Silberman. 2001. *The Bible Unearthed: Archaeology's New Vision of Ancient Israel and the Origin of Its Sacred Texts*. New York: Free Press. Interesting for the entire Bible and beyond is Akenson, Donald Harman. 1998. *Surpassing Wonder: The Invention of the Bible and the Talmuds*. New York: Harcourt Brace & Company. Because so many works on these subjects are available and the information I offer is not under contention among biblical scholars, I do not footnote extensively. Much of the information, and more, may be found in Cross, F. L. and E. A. Livingstone (eds.) *The Oxford Dictionary of the Christian Church*. Oxford: Oxford University Press. For ease of use, the dictionary is cross-referenced.
285. Williams 2001a, 31-62.
286. For others, see Williams 2001a, 36-40.
287. The modern Catholic *Catechism (Catechism of the Catholic Church.* 1994. Mahwah, New Jersey: Paulist Press) does not use the word "guilt" in its articles on original sin or baptism. However, the idea that original sin transmits guilt as well as our fallen nature dates to Tertullian (c.160-c.225) and is fully developed in Augustine (354-430). The Council of Sens (1140) condemned Abelard for not recognizing original sin as guilt. Modern individualism along with evolutionary theory undermines the whole idea, probably why Pope Pius XII in 1950 reaffirmed the essential role of Adam as a historical individual (Pius XII [1950] 1956. *Human Generis. The Papal Encyclicals in Their Historical Context.* (ed. Ann Fremantle, tr. Ronald A. Knox). New York: New American Library.) The confusion in paragraphs 404 and 405 of the Catholic *Catechism* stems from not explicitly naming guilt as a part of original sin. If human nature

alone is transmitted down the generations, infant guilt ceases to be a problem. The Catholic Church faces insurmountable difficulties in being infallible while, at the same time, needing to change its theology in the light of new discoveries. The catechism avoids the word while retaining the concept.

288. It always strikes me that, in crediting us with Jesus' grace without transformation, God saves by divine pretense.

289. Freiday, 67.

290. Freiday, 67.

291. Freiday, 69-70.

292. Freiday. 66-68.

293. Freiday, 66.

294. Williams 2001a, 60. I can find no reference in Quaker writings of the seventeenth century to the naturalness or unnaturalness of death. Douglas Gwyn, the great Fox scholar, knows of none, either (personal communication). Calvin says Adam's soul dies at the Fall, yet he also believes the Fall entails physical death. (See Calvin, John [1559] 1995. *Institutes of the Christian Religion* (tr. Henry Beveridge).Grand Rapids, Michigan: Wm. B. Eerdmans, Book II, chapter 1, paragraphs 5 and 6, I. pp. 214-15.) Perhaps the question simply was not an issue.

295. Again, the Eastern Church agrees with this reading. See Williams 2001a, 60.

296. Woolman, 208.

297. In Methodism, sanctification is possible, if rare. However, Methodism came not from Protestantism, but from the Anglican Church that retains much Catholic theology. Moreover, Quakerism influenced Methodism.

298. There are some minor exceptions.

299. Freiday, 72.

300. Freiday, 72.

301. Freiday, 88.

302. Freiday, 79.

303. Freiday, 77.

304. Freiday, 116.

305. Freiday, 83.

306. Freiday, 93.

307. Freiday, 125.

308. Freiday, 130-131.

309. Freiday, 131-33.

310. Sharman 1980, 75.

311. Gorman, 68.

312. Gwyn 1986, 93.

313. Gwyn 2004 in Dandelion, 144.

314. Probably the best discussion of the details, without too much minutiae, is Funk, Hoover, and the Jesus Seminar, 9-21.
315. Cooper, 16-17.
316. Cooper, 17.
317. See Williams 2001b, 44-54, for details of the scholarly consensus about the historical Jesus.
318. Cooper, 40.
319. Williams, Patricia A. 2003. "Jesus as a Friend." *Friends Journal* **49** (December), pp. 11-13, 35.
320. Josephus, Falvius. [c.94 C.E.] 1981. *The Complete Works of Josephus* (tr. William Whiston). Grand Rapids, Michigan: Kregel. The references are in *Antiquities of the Jews* XVIII. III. 3 and V. 2, respectively.
321. Scholarship on the last supper gives it every meaning imaginable. For a brief discussion, see Williams 2001b, 111-15.
322. Williams 2001a, 48-62.
323. Hamm, Thomas D. 2004. "'New Light on Old Ways': Gurneyites, Wilburites, and the Early Friends" in *George Fox's Legacy: Friends for 350 Years, Quaker History* **93**, #1 (Spring). Haverford, Pennsylvania: Friends Historical Association, pp. 53-67.
324. Freiday and Roberts, 59-65. I quote only from 59-62. The questions I quote are in bold in the original.
325. Freiday and Roberts, 33-4.
326. Cooper, 21.
327. Freiday, 46.
328. Fox, George. [1831] 1990. *The Works of George Fox, Vol. III. The Great Mystery.* State College, Pennsylvania: New Foundation Publications, 409.
329. Freiday, 47.
330. Fox 1990, Vol. I, 92-4; Vol. III, 410.
331. Freiday, 50.
332. Freiday, 61.
333. Freiday, 50. Penington, 3-10. And a German reformer predating the Quakers, Sebastian Frank. See Burdick, Winifred. 1986. "Sources of Universalism in Quaker Thought" in *The Quaker Universalist Reader Number 1: A Collection of Essays, Addresses and Lectures.* Landenberg, Pennsylvania: Quaker Universalist Fellowship, 56.
334. Freiday, 53-4.
335. Freiday, 59.
336. Cadbury, Henry Joel [1953] 1996. *A Quaker Approach to the Bible.* Landenberg, Pennsylvania: Quaker Universalist Fellowship, 10.
337. Freiday, 49.
338. Freiday, 64.

339. Freiday, 64.
340. Freiday, 64-65.
341. Freiday, 65.
342. Cadbury, 9.
343. Freiday, 56-57.
344. Freiday, 57.
345. Ehrman, Bart D. 1993. *The Orthodox Corruption of Scripture: The Effect of Early Christological Controversies on the Text of the New Testament.* New York: Oxford University Press.
346. Freiday, 56.
347. The Massoretic text is famous for the care with which it was copied from early times and, so, became the official text for Jews and the Latin Church. The Leningrad Codex is the oldest complete text of the Hebrew Scriptures, dating to about 1000 C.E. and housed in St. Petersburg (formerly Leningrad).
348. Hedrick, Charles W. 2002. "The Thirty-four Gospels: Diversity and Division Among the Earliest Christians. *Bible Review* **18** (3), 20-31,46-47.
349. For more information on this fascinating subject, see Ehrman, Bart D. 2003. *Lost Christianities: The Battles for Scripture and the Faiths We Never Knew.* Oxford: Oxford University Press.
350. My own translation, based on Douglas, J. D. (ed.) 1990. *The New Greek-English Interlinear New Testament* (tr. Robert K. Brown and Philip W. Comfort). Wheaton, Illinois: Tyndale House.
351. Barclay treats it as a fully spiritual, non-bodily event, following St. Paul. See Freiday and Roberts, 114.
352. An intellectual giant, he succeeded Isaac Newton in the Lucasian chair of mathematics at Cambridge.
353. See, especially, Miller, Robert J. 2003. *Born Divine: The Births of Jesus & Other Sons of God.* Santa Rosa, California: Polegridge Press.
354. In Sharman 1980, 91.
355. In Sharman 1980, 107.
356. In Sharman 1980, 115.
357. Fox 1990, Vol. I, 397. I have used the NRSV. Fox, of course, quotes the KJV.
358. In Ambler, 72.
359. I do not think science has proved anything, or can. However, others differ. Neuroscience has discovered an area in the brain that is active in practiced meditators. Its meaning is ambiguous and debated. See Newberg, Andrew, Eugene D'Aquili, and Vince Rause. 2001. *Why God Won't Go Away: Brain Science and the Biology of Belief.* New York: Random House, and Alper, Matthew. 2001. *The "God" Part of the Brain: A Scientific Interpretation of Human Spirituality and God.* Boulder, Colorado: Rogue Press.

360. In Ambler, 2.
361. Pym, 11.
362. Pym, 36.
363. Hick, John. 1986. "Christ in a Universe of Faith" in *The Quaker Universalist Reader Number 1: A Collection of Essays, Addresses and Lectures.* Landenberg, Pennsylvania: Quaker Universalist Fellowship, 31.
364. If my simplification seems to defame Protestantism, compare it with Calvin, Book II, Chapter I, Paragraphs 4-11 (I. pp. 212-220). The *Institutes* runs over one thousand pages, so quoting it briefly is difficult. Furthermore, the pages are numbered consecutively until the middle of Book III, to page 582, and then begin at 1, making reference difficult. Calvin writes of "innate corruption from the very womb" (I. p. 214) and "their [infants'] whole nature is, as it were, a seed-bed of sin, and therefore cannot but be odious and abominable to God. . . . This perversity in us never ceases" (I. p. 217-8). "Man is naturally hateful to God" (I. p. 220). He comments, "God was pleased to ordain that those gifts which he had bestowed on the first man, that man should lose as well for his descendants as for himself" (I. p. 216) and "God not only foresaw the fall of the first man, and in him the ruin of his posterity; but also at his own pleasure arranged it" (II. p. 232).
365. Friday, 73.
366. Friday, 75. See Calvin, Book III, Chapter XXIII, Paragraphs 7-10 (II. pp. 232-233). Intellectually, Calvin's argument is a mess, but he clearly places the responsibility on God: "The first man fell because the Lord deemed it meet that he should."
367. Friday, 77.
368. Friday, 77.
369. Friday, 127-8.
370. Friday, 129-30.
371. The Catholic Church says what Barclay claims. However, Catholicism is much more complex and interesting than this simplification implies. It agrees with the Quakers that people can cooperate with God toward their own salvation after God's initial prompting and concurs that some become saints, holy men and women. However, it considers sainthood rare, whereas the Quakers insist sanctification is possible for all.
Calvin, too, says much about grace, and the doctrine of imputed grace does call for growth of personal righteousness in the saved. If indications from Fox and Barclay are accurate, however, grace and righteousness were not being emphasized in Puritan pulpits. Moreover, the doctrine seems inconsistent. Calvin says explicitly that our nature has been "so corrupted, that mere cure is not

sufficient. There must be a new nature" (Calvin, Book II, Chapter II, paragraph 9, p. I. 219). If a person's nature is replaced, the essence is lost, so that person is not reformed; rather, another, the replacement, is! The logic of imputed grace is that the person to whom it is imputed remains corrupted.

372. Freiday, 72. Original in italics.
373. Quoted in Freiday, 113.
374. Freiday, 113.
375. Freiday, 114-5.
376. The whole argument is in Freiday, 83. I stole a moment of poetic license. Barclay says, "so close that salvation is near at hand."
377. Freiday, 100.
378. Freiday, 104-5.
379. Freiday, 87.
380. Freiday, 111.
381. Argument in Freiday, 111-2; quotations 112.
382. Freiday, 87.
383. Freiday, 254.
384. Fox 1997, 34.
385. Freiday, 115-21.
386. Quoted in Brinton 1973, 10.
387. In Sharman 1980, 113 and 120.
388. Brinton 1973, 10-19.
389. Brinton 1957, 17-20; quote, 17.
390. Gwyn 1986, 109. Also see Freiday, 106.
391. Given Catholicism's claim that only men can rule in the church, the masculine "kingdom" seems appropriate here.
392. Funk, Hoover, and the Jesus Seminar, 207.
393. Gwyn 1986, 15.
394. Brinton 2002, 263.
395. Peacocke, Arthur. 2001. *Paths from Science toward God: The End of All Our Exploring.* Oxford: Oneworld, 75.
396. Wilber, Ken. 1998. *The Marriage of Sense and Soul: Integrating Science and Religion.* New York: Broadway Books, 155-6.
397. Wilber.
398. Schwabe, Calvin W. 1999. *Quakerism and Science.* Wallingford, Pennsylvania: Pendle Hill (Pamphlet 343).
399. Gould, Stephen Jay. 1999. *Rock of Ages: Science and Religion in the Fullness of Life.* New York: Ballantine Publishing Group.
400. Henderson, Stephen. 2004. "Let there be Lasers: The Illumination of Charles Townes" in "Historic Milestones," Radnor, Pennsylvania: John Templeton Foundation, June.

401. In a letter to Robert Hooke dated 5 February 1676. Quoted in Knowles, Elizabeth (ed.). 2004. *Oxford Dictionary of Quotations.* Oxford: Oxford University Press.
402. Quoted in Peacocke, 7.
403. Capra, 34.
404. Capra, 36.
405. Capra, 306.
406. Peacocke, 30-1.
407. Brinton 2002, 170.
408. The point is clearly made by the famous astronomer and Quaker, Arthur Eddington in Eddington, Arthur Stanley. 1929. *Science and the Unseen World.* London: George Allen & Unwin Ltd., 45.
409. The suggestion is in Wilber, 20-21, and seems exactly right.
410. Ehrman, 2003. An excellent discussion of orthodoxy and heresy runs from pages 163-179.
411. Ambler, 178. Open cultures clearly pose many difficulties for religions. If being open to experiments on issues of religious truth raised problems for authoritarian religions, being open to moral experimentation create dilemmas for sects like the Quakers, who also seceded for a time.
412. For excellent discussions, see Chaisson, Eric J. 2001. *Cosmic Evolution: The Rise of Complexity in Nature.* Cambridge, Mass: Harvard University Press and Smolin, Lee. 1997. *The Life of the Cosmos.* New York: Oxford University Press.
413. See Capra, 189-94.
414. Wilbur, 213.
415. For more detail, see Williams, Patricia A. (forthcoming). *Revealing God: A New Theology from Science and Jesus.* Helpful on cosmology are Greene, Brian. 1999. *The Elegant Universe: Superstrings, Hidden Dimensions, and the Quest for the Ultimate Theory.* New York: W. W. Norton & Company, Gribbin, John and Mary. 2000. *Stardust: Supernovae and Life – The Cosmic Connection.* New Haven: Yale University Press, and Smolin. On evolution, see the first sixty pages of Rachels, James. 1991. *Created from Animals: The Moral Implications of Darwinism.* New York: Oxford University Press or my *Doing without Adam and Eve,* chapter seven, and Lewin, Roger. 1998. *Principles of Human Evolution: A Core Textbook.* Oxford: Blackwell.
416. In Davies, Paul. 1999. *The Fifth Miracle: The Search for the Origin and Meaning of Life.* New York: Simon and Schuster. Davies argues that there are deep philosophical and religious ramifications to whether life originated once as an accident or whether its origin is built into the laws of the universe. His conclusion is, we do not know.

417. Dyson, Freeman J. 2002. "Science & Religion: No Ends in Sight" in *The New York Review of Books* **49** (March 28), 4.
418. See Williams, Patricia A. (forthcoming). "How Evil Entered the World: An Exploration through Deep Time" in Hewlett, Martinez and Ted Peters (eds.). *The Evolution of Evil*. Vandenhoeck and Ruprecht.
419. Freiday, throughout. See especially 152-7.
420. Murphy, Nancey. 1998. "Human Nature: Historical, Scientific and Religious Issues" in Brown, Warren S., Nancey Murphy, and H. Newton Malony (eds.). *Whatever Happened to the Soul? Scientific and Theological Portraits of Human Nature*. Minneapolis: Fortress, 6-7.
421. See Dennett, Daniel C. 1991. *Consciousness Explained*. Boston: Little, Brown and Company and, on the other side, McGinn, Colin. 1999. *The Mysterious Flame: Conscious Minds in a Material World*. New York: Basic Books.
422. Brown, Warren S. 1998. "Cognitive Contributions to the Soul" in Brown et al., 100.
423. Borg, Marcus J. 1994. *Jesus in Contemporary Scholarship*. Valley Forge, Pennsylvania: Trinity, 174-8.
424. Jones, Rufus M. 1941. *Spirit in Man*. Stanford, California: Stanford University Press, mentioned in the "Forward" by Elton Trueblood, p. x.
425. *Catechism*, item 364.
426. Under a Greek/Roman/Hebrew understanding of conception, the virgin birth is possible because the woman supplies the flesh, the man the spirit. Thus, the gods or the Holy Spirit can supply the spirit, and Jesus be a divine-human. But today we know DNA is a chemical that male and female contribute equally to engender a child. If God supplies the divine spirit, but forgets the DNA, no child can develop. But if God supplies human DNA, the child will develop, but not be divine. Therefore, no virgin birth.
427. Polkinghorne, John. 2003. "Physics and Metaphysics in a Trinitarian Perspective" in *Theology and Science* 1 (April), 33-49.
428. Polkinghorne, John. 2002. *The God of Hope and the End of the World*. New Haven: Yale University Press. Reviewed, with insight, by famous physicist, Freeman J. Dyson, above, 4-6.
429. *Theology and Science*, 2004 **2** (April) and (October). The results of the project are summarized in Wildman, Wesley J. 2004. "The Divine Action Project, 1988-2003" in *Theology and Science* 2 (April), 31-75.
430. Murphy, Nancey and George F. R. Ellis. 1996. *On the Moral Nature of the Universe: Theology, Cosmology, and Ethics*. Minneapolis: Fortress.
431. Hefner, Philip. 1993. *The Human Factor: Evolution, Culture, and Religion*. Minneapolis, Fortress, especially 131-8.

432. Davies, Paul. 1998. "Is the Universe Absurd?" in Peters, Ted. *Science and Theology: The New Consonance*. Boulder Colorado: Westview, 74-5.

433. Murphy 1998, 21.

434. Jones, Rufus M. 1904/23. *Social Law in the Spiritual World: Studies in Human and Divine Interrelationship*. New York: Swarthmore. 1936. *The Testimony of the Soul*. New York: Macmillan, 170-173. 1941.

435. See (in alphabetical order) Damasio, Antonio R. 1994. *Descartes' Error: Emotion, Reason, and the Human Brain*. New York: G. P. Putnam's Sons. Damasio 1999. *The Feeling of What Happens: Body and Emotion in the Making of Consciousness*. New York: Harcourt Brace and Company. Edelman, Gerald M. and Guilio Tononi. 2000. *A Universe of Consciousness: How Matter Becomes Imagination*. New York: Basic Books. Feinberg, Todd E. 2001. *Altered Egos: How the Brain Creates the Self*. Oxford: Oxford University Press. Greenfield, Susan. 2000. *The Private Life of the Brain: Emotions, Consciousness, and the Secret of the Self*. New York: John Wiley & Sons. Llinas, Rodolfo R. 2001. *I of the Vortex: From Neurons to Self*. Cambridge, Mass.: MIT Press. Newberg and D'Aquila. Ornstein, Robert 1993. *The Roots of the Self: Unraveling the Mystery of Who We Are*. San Francisco: HarperSanFrancisco. Siegel, Daniel J. 1999. *The Developing Mind: Toward a Neurobiology of Interpersonal Experience*. New York: Guilford.

436. Clifford, Anne M. 1998. "Biological Evolution and the Human Soul: A Theological Proposal for Generationism" in Peters 1998, 169-70.

437. Dillenberger, John. 1960. *Protestant Thought and Natural Science: A Historical Interpretation*. Notre Dame, Indiana: University of Notre Dame Press, 229.

438. Peters, Ted and Martinez Hewlett. 2003. *Evolution from Creation to New Creation: Conflict, Conversation, and Convergence*. Nashville: Abingdon Press, 159.

439. Haught, John F. 2000. *God after Darwin: A Theology of Evolution*. Boulder, Colorado: Westview.

440. One recent issue is almost entirely devoted to religious naturalism and features some of its strongest supporters. See *Zygon: Journal of Religion & Science*. 2003, **38** (March).

441. See Boyer, Pascal. 2001. *Religion Explained: The Evolutionary Origins of Religions Thought*. New York: Basic Books and Wilson, David Sloan. 2002. *Darwin's Cathedral: Evolution, Religion, and the Nature of Society*. Chicago: University of Chicago Press.

442. Reviewed, as always with her acerbic humor, in Midgley, Mary. 1992. *Science as Salvation: A Modern Myth and Its Meaning*. London: Routledge.

443. Peacocke, Arthur. 2000. "Science and the Future of Theology: Critical Issues" in *Zygon: Journal of Religion & Science* 35, 119-140.

444. Peacocke, Arthur. 1984. *Intimations of Reality: Critical Realism in Science and Religion*. Notre Dame, Indiana: University of Notre Dame Press, 47-50. Quotation page 50.

445. For corresponding sayings, see Borg, Marcus and Ray Riegert (eds.). 1997. *Jesus and Buddha: The Parallel Sayings*. Berkeley, California: Seastone.

446. Peacocke, Arthur. 1993. *Theology for a Scientific Age: Being and Becoming – Natural, Divine, and Human* (Enlarged Edition). Minneapolis: Fortress, 228-334.

447. The simple formula must be supplemented with details to predict unusual social behavior correctly.

448. This is a simplified model, complicated somewhat by real-world details. For a full explanation, see the eminent comprehensive text, Wilson, Edward O. 1975. *Sociobiology: The New Synthesis*. Cambridge, Mass.: Belknap.

449. See Alcock, John. 2001. *The Triumph of Sociobiology*. Oxford: Oxford University Press.

450. For a major textbook, see Buss, David M. 1999. *Evolutionary Psychology: The New Science of the Mind*. Boston: Allyn and Bacon.

451. Gould, Stephen Jay. 1994. "So Near and Yet So Far" in *New York Review of Books* 41, 17 (October 20), 24-28.

452. Ridley, Matt. 1996. *The Origins of Virtue: Human Instincts and the Evolution of Cooperation*. New York: Penguin, 129.

453. Cases of reciprocity among animals of lesser intelligence are observed, but rarely.

454. For a brief review of the dispositions arising from reciprocity, see Irons, William. 2004. "An Evolutionary Critique of the Created Co-Creator Concept" in *Zygon* 39 (December), 778-87. The quotation is on 778.

455. Schwartz, Jeffrey M. and Sharon Begley. 2002. *The Mind and the Brain: Neuroplasticity and the Power of Mental Force*. New York: ReganBooks.

456. Freiday, 37.

457. Freiday, 205-6.

458. Hayden, Brian. 2003. *Shamans, Sorcerers, and Saints: A Prehistory of Religion*. Washington: Smithsonian Books, 238-9.

459. Sharman 1980, xiii.

460. Freiday, 67-68.

461. In Ambler, 89-90 and Freiday, 430, respectively

462. Freiday, 261-2 and 296.

463. Brinton 2002, 251.

464. Freiday, 68 and 430.

465. Jones 1936, 153-4.

466. Singer, Peter. 1981. *The Expanding Circle: Ethics and Sociobiology.* New York: Farrar, Straus & Giroux. Writing before human sociobiology morphed into evolutionary psychology, Singer argues that reason forces us to move from the narrow circle of affection for our relatives to due regard for the interests of all humankind, and even to those of other animals.

467. Dawkins, Richard. 1976. *The Selfish Gene.* New York: Oxford University Press. There are numerous examples aside from Dawkins. Unrelieved selfishness is one of the repeated themes of many who write on sociobiology. I think they distort the evidence.

468. They ignore ideological evil, as in the Third Reich, unless they incorporate our symbolic and metaphoric capacities. With these included, Hitler's characterization of the Jews as evil, pests, vermin, cancers, etc. destroying the German people and best eliminated for the salvation of Germany becomes explicable. Not exculpable, but explicable.

469. For a less schematic, but still simple description, see Williams 2001a, 48-62.

470. It is grounded in Aristotelian psychology, notably not a Christian.

471. Damasio 1999.

472. Peacocke 2001, 80.

473. Mitchell, Stephen (tr. and ed.). 1988. *Tao Te Ching.* New York: HarperPerennial, saying 25.

474. Mitchell, saying 32.

475. A Bodhisattva is, more or less, a Buddhist saint. A Bodhisattva seeks enlightenment but, on the threshold of Nirvana, returns to the world to save others.

476. Mitchell, saying 39.

477. Burke, T. Patrick. 1996. *The Major Religions: An Introduction with Texts.* Cambridge, Mass.: Blackwell, 167.

478. Mitchell, saying 37.

479. Mitchell, saying 32.

480. Edelman, Gerald M. 2004. *Wider than the Sky: The Phenomenal Gift of Consciousness.* New Haven: Yale University Press, 78-81.

481. Turner, Mark. 1996. *The Literary Mind.* New York: Oxford University Press, 51.

482. Lakoff, George and Mark Johnson. 1980. *Metaphors We Live By.* Chicago: University of Chicago Press, 24.

483. Lakoff, George and Mark Johnson. 1999. *Philosophy in the Flesh: The Embodied Mind and Its Challenge to Western Thought.* New York. Basic Books.
484. Lakoff and Johnson, 1999.
485. Lakoff and Johnson, 1980, 15-22.
486. Turner, 14-15.
487. Turner.
488. Lakoff and Johnson 1999, 569-583.
489. Cooper, Wilmer A. 1990. *A Living Faith: An Historical Study of Quaker Beliefs.* Richmond, Indiana: Friends United Press, 12.
490. The word *God* is probably not a metaphor, but a name, as Yahweh is a name.
491. Fox, 11.
492. Freiday, 254.
493. Freiday, 28.
494. Dunn, James D. G. 1975. *Jesus and the Spirit: A Study of the Religious and Charismatic Experience of Jesus and the First Christians as Reflected in the New Testament.* London: SCM Press Ltd., 201.
495. Capra, Fritjof. 2000. *The Tao of Physics: An Exploration of the Parallels between Modern Physics and Eastern Mysticism* (4th Edition, updated). Boston: Shambhala, p. 24.
496. Stace, W. T. 1960. *Mysticism and Philosophy.* Los Angeles: Jeremy P. Tarcher, Inc., 61-62.
497. Stace, 109-123.
498. Stace. Also see Underhill, Evelyn. [1911] 1990. *Mysticism: The Preeminent Study in the Nature and Development of Spiritual Consciousness.* New York: Doubleday.
499. Freiday, 19.
500. Benson.
501. Sharman 1991, 98.
502. Gwyn, Douglas. 2004. "Apocalypse Now and Then: Reading Early Friends in the Belly of the Beast" in Dandelion, Pink (ed.). *The Creation of Quaker Theory: Insider Perspectives.* Burlington, Vermont: Ashgate, pp. 132-3.
503. Skinner and Stillwell, 32-34.
504. Skinner and Stillwell, 42.
505. Letter dated London, 25th or 30th day, 3rd month, 1675 in Skinner and Stillwell, 100.
506. Fox, George [1831] 1990. *The Works of George Fox, Vol. IV. The Doctrinals, Vol. I.* State College, Pennsylvania: New Foundation Publications, 41-42.
507. Ambler, Rex (ed.). 2001. *Truth of the Heart: An Anthology of George Fox 1624-1691.* London. Quaker Books, 46.

508. In a letter dated 22nd day, 9th month, 1682, in Sharman, Cecil W. (ed.). 1980. *No More but My Love: Letters of George Fox 1624-1691*. London: Quaker Home Service, 118. In the seventeenth century, a plantation was a planting of people.
509. Hicks, Elias, 439.
510. Freiday, 340.
511. Freiday, 341.
512. Freiday, 163-4.
513. Freiday, 438.

INDEX

CPSIA information can be obtained at www.ICGtesting.com
Printed in the USA
LVOW061820041011

249072LV00001B/62/P